Talk Reform

Primary Socialization, Language & Education
Edited by Basil Bernstein
University of London Institute of Education
Sociological Research Unit

Talk Reform

Explorations in Language
for Infant School Children

D M & G A Gahagan

Foreword by Basil Bernstein

LONDON ROUTLEDGE & KEGAN PAUL

First published 1970
by Routledge & Kegan Paul Ltd
Broadway House, 68–74 Carter Lane
London E.C.4
Printed in Great Britain
by Clarke, Doble & Brendon Ltd
Plymouth
ISBN 0 7100 6875 1

Contents

Foreword

Basil Bernstein

In this monograph, Georgina and Denis Gahagan set out in detail the exploratory language enquiry which was carried out in a group of schools in a predominantly working class area of London.

The reader should bear in mind that the programme began in 1964 when we had few precedents to go on in this country. It was set up under conditions that were far from ideal. It constituted only a small part of the total research effort under my direction. I did, in fact, have severe doubts about the desirability of running any language programme at all. On the one hand, a strong case could be made out for field-testing some of the more important educational implications of my work. I felt, however, that the design and execution and evaluation of such a programme was a complex project in its own right. I was also uneasy about the methodological consequence of running such a programme in an area which was already marked out for other (more distinctly sociological) enquiries. These misgivings were eventually outweighed by the feeling that the attempt to run a language programme could hardly fail to be informative. Since little was known about the problems involved in setting up and implementing such programmes, useful practical knowledge was certain to be gained. This was also the feeling of officials of the then Ministry of Education, who were extremely anxious to see a trial language programme implemented.

As the Gahagans say in their book, we were a little worried as we did not want to interfere with the children's acquisition of basic skills, and also all of us were aware of how exploratory the whole endeavour was. For this reason, the programme was limited to twenty minutes a day. The resources made available for the programme and its execution and evaluation represented only a very small percentage of the Unit's total resources. For example, at one time the Unit consisted of five linguists, four sociologists and ancillary help, but only two psychologists. The two psychologists, Georgina and Denis Gahagan, were not simply concerned with the language programme but also supervised all psychological testing carried out on the children for the life of the project. Indeed, when the project started in the summer of 1964 it was administered by only one psychologist, Denis Gahagan. Georgina was appointed to share in the work only in the spring of 1965.

It is difficult to give the reader an idea of just how much work the programme required, or, indeed, of the many anxieties to which it gave rise. The Gagahans together designed an incredible amount of material and equipment. In nearly all cases they started from scratch. The various series of picture stories had to be thought out, drawn and supplied to the teachers along with the vocabulary lists which they requested. The fortnightly seminar required considerable planning, and the listening to the tape-recorded discussion of the teachers was sometimes a morning's work. In addition, there were regular visits to each of the three schools in order to get an idea of the problems the teachers were facing in its implementation. At one time we felt that we were being defeated by the architecture of the schools, which created problems of floor space. The Gahagans designed a balcony for each classroom which would take advantage of their height and release the pressure on space on the floor of the class. This design was submitted to the L.E.A. and to the Ministry of Education. Unfortunately, the alteration was approved too late for incorporation in the project. I mention it only to show the total commitment of the Gahagans and the range of problems encountered during the lifetime of the project.

I must also point out that the Gahagans developed their programme very much in terms of how they saw the problem. My own work was no more than a starting point and probably offered little except vague generalizations. I do not intend to say very much about their programme, as its description and criticism will be found in the text. In many respects it aimed at an all round experience relying much upon the setting up of special contexts, often in the form of games, which would encourage the children to explore through language different orders of meaning. The Gagahans did not wholly eschew using a didactic approach, but equally there were many opportunities where more self or group regulated approaches were used. It seems to me that the approach one uses is not an absolute but depends upon the particular problem or even upon a particular stage of the development of the problem.

Throughout the programme, after the first six months, a number of attempts were made to evaluate its effects. The Gahagans spend much time in their book explaining the problems involved. In many cases we do not know whether an initial gain in some skill was more developed later or whether an initial gain was lost later. It may well be that if we had had more time and personnel a more extensive range of evaluation experiments would have been designed, closely linked with the general aims as well as with the specific tasks of the programme.

On the whole the evaluation enquiries fall into two groups. Enquiries into the children's performances upon tasks that were indirectly related to their classroom learning experience (like the paired-associate experiment) and evaluations which appear to be more directly related to the classroom experience (like the English Attainment Test). The Gahagans have included both kinds of evaluation.

Clearly, given the conditions under which the Gahagans worked, their results are both suggestive and distinctly encouraging. In the general area of discrimination and classification, in the verbal coding of sensory experience, in the development of inter-personal forms of control, the language programme children, on the whole, are superior to the non-language programme children. Perhaps the most important result of the Gahagans' work is the result of the English Attainment Test given at the end of the project, which shows most clearly the benefits of the language programme for both white and West Indian children.

These results are most encouraging in view of the fact that the programme was only a twenty-minute a day activity. What would be possible, if a more systematic, more inclusive approach was followed in which we could consider the day as the unit and the time period the whole of the primary stage? It is a little presumptuous to be certain about the abilities of children when there exists no theory of an optimum learning environment and, even if there were, the funds to create it on the scale required would not be . forthcoming.

The study described in this book should be examined bearing in mind the terms of the project within which the Gahagans were to work. These were:

(1) To produce a programme which involved no costly equipment other than equipment which was within the range of the infant school budget.

(2) A total expenditure on materials of only £300 over the three years.

(3) A programme which took only twenty minutes a day and which in no way would affect the children's learning of other skills.

(4) To support the teachers and work through the daily problems which they inevitably found in carrying out the programme.

(5) To provide continuously over two and a half years the materials required.

(6) To design, administer and analyse a diverse group of evaluations.

(7) To take responsibility for the administration and analysis of the Unit's general psychological testing of all sample children.

There are many problems raised by attempts to create new educational environments. In this book the Gahagans have set out their own view both of the problem and of its possible solution. My own feeling is that their book represents the first systematic attempt of researchers in this country to work with teachers over a two and a half year period in order to assist in the daily problems of the education of children.

Finally, it would seem that the teachers have been over-looked in this introduction. On the contrary, the teachers at every step in the work advised, criticized and actively helped in the design of much of the material. In the end, whatever the benefits are to the children, they were made possible because of the teachers.

Preface

This research project was initiated some five years ago. Particularly in the early stages all members of the Sociological Research Unit spent many hours discussing questions of the design and nature of the programme. Their contributions were central and invaluable to the research as a whole. Throughout the project we have been indebted to everyone who made suggestions and criticisms and we would like to thank them here. In addition, we would like to thank personally Professor Basil Bernstein who initiated and designed the project and who provided constant encouragement, stimulating ideas and valuable criticisms.

We acknowledge our debt to the Local Education Authority whose generosity and imaginativeness made this project possible. We cannot praise too highly the head teachers who managed to accommodate our invasions and requests over a period of three years with unfailing calm and good humour. Central to the success of the project were the class teachers who administered the programme and who attended the seminars. To them we extend our warmest thanks and appreciation.

We were assisted in data collection and analysis by Doris Higgins and Bunty Mitchell to whom we are extremely grateful. Throughout the entire project we depended on Rosalind Greenbaum for her immensely efficient and unstinting secretarial help.

D.M.G. and G.A.G.
Sociological Research Unit
Institute of Education
University of London

Chapter 1   Who's for Tennis?

Verbal encounters with others frequently do not run as we intend them to. Sometimes simply phrased requests for simple information yield inadequate replies or replies to different questions. Discussions and arguments often end in an awareness that we do not 'speak the same language' as one another. These observations are particularly true of encounters with people of rather different social class or group membership to ourselves. There occurs what is commonly called 'a break-down in communication'. The following examples show communications which never really got off the ground.

I: A customer approaches a young assistant behind the sports counter in a large store. The customer is anxious to buy some inexpensive tennis balls. All the tennis balls on display vary considerably in price, with one particular brand of ball being remarkably cheap. The customer asks the assistant why these balls are so much cheaper than the others. The following conversation ensues:

> *Assistant:* Well like for practice—you know—championship
>   and that—you can knock about a bit.
> *Customer:* Are they made of some different material?
> *Assistant:* Well like for practice—you know for a championship
>   against a wall like—they're alright.
> *Customer:* They would stand up to an ordinary game?
> *Assistant:* Well they're practice ones like—championship—
>   you can knock about a bit you know.

II: The task for the speaker in the next example was rather more difficult. He has been asked not for fairly simple information but for his opinion in a discussion on the abolition of capital punishment. The following sequence is an example of his contribution:

> It's all according like well those youths and that if they get
> with gangs and that they most have a bit of a lark around and
> say it goes wrong and that they probably knock some off I

1

think they do it just to be a bit big you know getting
publicity here and there.

III: In the last example a college girl is asked by an interviewer,
'What kind of a person is X?' (the college girl's best friend). The
college girl's description runs as follows:

> Mary is a girl friend back in—— We went to school together
> for one year. She is about five feet six inches tall, and has
> red hair. She's a lot of fun. She has a real good sense of
> humour; she's fun to be with; she's real smart. She plays
> musical instruments.[1]

The reader must make allowances when reading the first two
examples as they are transcripts from recorded speech, and probably look more incoherent than they actually sounded. Our most
eloquent sequences can appear amazingly disjointed when transcribed. What is characteristic about these three scraps of speech?
One characteristic they all have in common is that they are inadequate with respect to what the listener wants. For example, in the
first instance, the assistant might not have known the answer to the
customer's question, and realizing this, referred him to someone
who did. If he did know the answer, then it should have been
given in terms of the material from which the tennis balls were
made, their durability, their performance under various conditions,
and so on. In fact, the assistant appeared not to understand the
question and, even though he did have *an* answer, he seemed to
be unable to utilize the usual syntactic devices for producing a
logically coherent sequence. We cannot believe that the task was
beyond the intelligence of this shop assistant. In the second example
the task was more difficult. However, since this speech sample
occurred during a study of verbal behaviour, we happen to know
that this contributor had an average I.Q. Again he appears to have
misunderstood the question, that is, whether he was for or against
capital punishment; and once again, he is not linking the various
elements contained in his argument in a logical order.

The last example, which has admittedly been punctuated, is not
logically incoherent as the first two were. However, if we consider
the rich vocabulary of description and qualification available for
presenting a personality of which we have considerable experience,
then this description is rather meagre. It did not in fact answer
the interviewer's question. Although we were not present on the
scene of these three conversations, it seems likely that the speakers
supplemented their poor verbal communication with a good deal of
gesture and intonation which is lost to us. They were using other
additional means of transmitting their meanings.

In summary then the speakers were not adapting their speech to the requirement of the listener, and they were scarcely exploiting those resources which a language system offers for conveying meanings. There are a number of questions however which we would like to raise. For instance, we would like to know whether this speech was typical for these speakers. If it were, then we would want to know if it were typical for more than a few rather incompetent individuals. In fact, one cannot definitely answer the questions about these particular speakers. We could, however, present samples of speech collected in many different situations which would be classified as similar to these examples. Supposing, however, such use of language was common and the speakers were restricted to these meagre verbal resources. What would be the consequences? The immediate consequences in two of the above examples were frustration and irritation on the part of the questioner, probably a vague sense of inadequacy on the part of the speakers and a deterioration in the potential social relation. The more general consequences of such restrictions could, however, be more serious. For one thing the language offered in these examples is not the language of public formal communication. News on radio and television and in the newspapers is presented very differently. This is not the kind of language used in Government offices, doctors' surgeries, hospitals or Citizens' Advice Bureaux. What happens to the individual whose only mode of communication is so very different from that of agencies which may be important to him at various times during his life? Clearly he is at a disadvantage in the system. He will fail to make known his precise needs, wishes and meanings, and the agency will probably be rather casual about trying to divine them.

The more socially adept and successful members of the population tailor their verbal strategies to fit the requirements of different situations that they encounter. Our power to deal successfully with many agencies, particularly formal or bureaucratic ones, depends almost entirely on the successful manipulation of language. For example, you might believe that your child had some abnormality which was holding him back at school. Your presentation of relevant evidence and suppression of irrelevant anecdote might determine whether or not the case was speedily investigated. Knowing with what degree of deference to address a policeman during a motoring incident could make the difference between a fine and the exchange of a few jokes. Your ability to convey the sense of abandonment and isolation of an elderly relative entering hospital might enable you to take advantage of rights that she might be too miserable to even ask for. Probably no one reading this book has ever or is ever likely to lack the verbal formulae which make life run fairly efficiently and, if these examples may seem over-charged, we would return the reader in that case to our customer in search of tennis balls.

Of course, one could argue that it is not sufficient to possess a number of verbal formulae. Surely having relevant knowledge and intelligence is even more important? Suppose it were the case, though, that these two factors, knowledge and intelligence, them-selves depended on one having had an adequate language system from the earliest years. Perhaps at this point we should declare our intentions. We do believe that the development of intelligence and the acquisition of knowledge are to a large extent dependent on our starting off with reasonable verbal resources.

School is an agency which so far we have ignored in our discus-sion. Yet school is an agency where different varieties of a common language are employed by staff and children, overwhelmingly so in schools situated in working-class areas. We have ignored the school as an agency until now because it is going to be the main focus of our attention. School is where a great deal of our knowledge is acquired and evidence from such studies as Douglas's *The Home and the School*[2] suggests that some of our measured intelligence is acquired there too.

For the five year old child with inappropriate language skills the teacher may well appear an incomprehensible and unpredictable individual who sets unreasonable tasks; that barely understanding the subtleties of 'because', 'if', 'sometimes', and 'perhaps', or the point of such qualifications as 'paler', 'medium', 'reddish', 'slightly', and so on, he could hardly be expected to base much learning on them or, for that matter, be expected to learn to read them. If we normally listened to speech that was heavily dependent on situa-tional referents and always emphasized with gesture and illustration, we would not be too good at listening to simple stories read aloud, let alone fairly abstract explanations. School might soon become a place where one switched off and dropped out and the spiral of under-achievement would have begun. Subsequent tests of intelli-gence would measure the results of this sequence of events as much as any genetic endowment. We do believe that this spiral of dis-advantagement is based on inadequate language early in life. The project to be described in later chapters was an attempt to produce a programme which could be used by teachers to combat this insidious form of disadvantage.

So far we have talked about language at the level of casual observation. In order to embark on a research project, clearly some-thing a little more rigorous is needed. We turn now to the work which has formulated these observations and ideas that we have been discussing into a complex and elaborate theory, that is, to the work of Basil Bernstein. We shall, of course, rather oversimplify the complexities and elaborations, and the reader should in any case refer to the original papers.[3] We want to select particular aspects of the theory which influenced the design and content of our language enrichment programme. Bernstein's theory has been set out in a number of papers during the last ten years. Some of the papers are purely theoretical and some of them report actual studies. The terms used in the theory have changed a little since the early papers. However, the essence of what Bernstein has said seems to us to have remained unchanged. Let us first list some of his major propositions.

Firstly, he suggests that within a common language two distinct modes of speech can be isolated, and that different *types* of social relations evoke these different modes of speech; that both types of social relations and their accompanying modes of speech can be distinguished and formally described; that members of certain social classes will tend to be restricted to a particular *type* of social relation and therefore to a particular form of speech; and finally that this restriction in terms of the current educational demands has negative consequences for them. We will examine each of these points in turn.

It is possible to identify social situations where the members know each other rather well, where membership of the group is self-consciously held, and where the meaning and intentions of the speakers and the understanding of the listeners can be largely taken for granted. A family gathering at Christmas or the meeting of a teenage gang would exemplify such a social situation. The important feature here is that the social group or gathering is the major focus of attention rather than the individual. A sense of solidarity is somehow imposed upon the members, and the major vehicle for its expression is the language that is used during such an encounter. For example, expression of private individual feelings and opinions tends to be suppressed by members in favour of words which have a communal meaning. We might try to imagine a conversation among a group of hippies living together. There might be a frequent occurrence of such phrases as 'There's no Vietnam when you're high, man!', a phrase familiar to all present and one which would symbolize the group membership—but rather few items like 'I am worried about the degree to which my political protest really reflects my political beliefs!' The difference here is not only one of simplicity of thought. These two remarks emphasize differentially the group and the individual. These situations are both

B

intimate yet impersonal. They are intimate because so little needs to be made explicit. Shared jokes and shared references evoke immediate responses. They are impersonal because individuals feel constrained against presenting private idiosyncratic information. A warm and cosy feeling is generated without individuals coming very close to each other's private meanings. The situation pre-supposes intimacy, that is, that individuals all know what everyone is talking about, but at the same time the situation prevents differences between individuals being made verbally explicit.

In general a transcript of all the speech in this kind of situation would probably reveal certain features. There would be references which were not explicit and therefore did not make sense to the outsider, although they would to the group. There would be sequences of speech of very simple, possibly very poor, constructions. There might well be big logical gaps between sequences. There would be a lot of repetition of a few words rather than use of a variety of different words. The transcript would reveal speech that was in certain ways rather similar to that observed in our two opening examples. However, as the reader will have noticed, these examples did not occur in social situations of the kind we have described. In at least two of these examples the listeners were very much strangers. Our speakers were then in fact using a language which the situation did not demand, and more than that, for which it was totally inappropriate. We suggest that these individuals were limited in their speech resources to the kind of speech which they actually produced in these examples. We shall be returning to this point shortly for major discussion.

To deepen our appreciation of the relationship between situational requirements and speech, let us take another example. The situation that follows is the exact opposite of the one we have just described. A tribunal, consisting of individuals, strangers to each other, holding widely varying skills, knowledge and view points, have met to consider the best way to evacuate and rehabilitate a small community in danger from a faulty reservoir. Each individual is necessary, since he has some unique skill or knowledge that no other member has. Furthermore, each individual sees the situation differently and has a different set of priorities in his solution of the problem. Each individual is called upon to speak. Each one must present his facts in a way that the others can understand. He must support his proposals with arguments designed to undermine the possible opposition. He must monitor carefully the reactions of his audience, and they must in turn follow his contribution with extreme care in order to make full use of the information. In this case speech on the transcript would appear much more like written language. Rules of grammar would be observed. Items would be presented in some degree of logical sequence. For example, one member of the tribunal might be a lawyer concerned with government compensation for loss of private property. He would be careful to explain the law on compensation rights *in general* before presenting complex arguments about how the law would apply in this particular instance. He would be choosing words carefully and he would probably use a very wide range of words and constructions. Some of his clause structures might be rather complex. In general, however, the language would be such that any literate Englishman could easily understand the transcript. This is rather an extreme and optimistic example; rather of how a tribunal ought to operate than of how they actually do operate. It is included here as a model—the antithesis of the first example.

The styles of language which would emerge in these two situations we have described would be distinctive, and they would correspond to the two codes made famous by Bernstein. The first would generate examples of restricted code; the second would generate examples of elaborated code. We have suggested that the style of language would be a distinctive one. This brings us to a problem. Is it possible to identify samples of speech outside the situation in which they were produced? Could one pick up a speech transcript and say definitely that it was an example of an elaborated or of a restricted code? We are not interested here in pronunciation or accent; we are looking rather for a characteristic vocabulary and grammatical structure which distinguishes elaborated from restricted code. In an early study Bernstein examined samples of speech collected in a situation which required the use of an elaborated code and was able to point out some formal characteristics of the restricted code.[4] He found, for example, that such speech contained fewer uncommon adjectives, adverbs and conjunctions; it contained fewer subordinate clauses, complex verb stems and fewer verbs in the passive voice. He also noticed a higher incidence of what he called socio-centric sequences such as 'You know', 'Isn't it'. (These are interesting devices for enforcing agreement upon the listener. In certain situations we have discussed, such agreement has peculiar social relevance.) Finally, he noticed little use of such phrases as 'I think', and of personal pronouns generally. Now, although this is encouraging, it is not the final solution to the problem of identifying codes within a language. Because, when we speak, our choice of words and phrases is so wide, we cannot easily generalize from one speech sample to a whole code. In Bernstein's study he did not use very many subjects nor sample their speech in a number of situations. (Indeed, the minimum number of subjects and situations required to generalize one's findings has yet to be agreed upon.) We cannot be certain therefore that these are the necessary defining characteristics of something called a restricted code. Secondly, how different must speech samples be in order to be classified as exemplifying separate codes? Let us suppose, for example, that we were interested in the dialect spoken in some remote country region. If, apart from accent and pronunciation, the only grammatical difference from the parent language was a variation on the use of the verb 'to be', and the only lexical difference was an extra word denoting 'hay', would we be justified in regarding this as a distinct dialect? There is a somewhat similar problem with Bernstein's code. How few uncommon adjectives, adverbs and conjunctions; how few subordinate clauses, complex verb stems and verbs in the passive voice do we have to have to be able to say that this sample of speech is a variant of a restricted code? A great deal of work has already been carried out with a view to finding a formal description which will pinpoint differences betwen restricted codes and elaborated codes, and for this we refer the reader to another paper in this series.[5]

Bernstein has indicated that *context* is a major control upon syntactic and lexical selections, consequently it is not easy to give general linguistic criteria for realizations of forms of speech which are variants of restricted code or elaborated code. For example, the form of a short, pithy summary of a long article may well be realized through a simple syntax and vocabulary, *but* the ability to produce such a summary may well point to the underlying regulations of an elaborated code rather than a restricted code. This example highlights the impossibility of assigning a particular stretch of speech or writing to the regulation of an elaborated code or restricted code without a *prior* knowledge of the context and role relationships which generate the speech or writing. Much of the Unit's work has been concerned with the creation of a range of contexts in order to examine social differences in the patterning of speech.

At this stage we are satisfied that there is a form of contextually controlled language which is both sparse in vocabulary and loose in structure, but we must wait for a more formal and academic definition of restricted codes and elaborated codes.

Let us at this point summarize the theory so far. We have illustrated the notion that certain social situations have important consequences for the speech which is generated in them. We have discussed the problem of describing language in general, and that of describing two forms of speech or code within a common language in particular.

We all encounter situations in which group reference is particularly important and we all, at these times, use a variant of a restricted code. Probably the most common setting for this experience is initially within the family, but later with peer groups, work groups, and so on. This brings us to a further major proposition of the Bernstein thesis. He suggests that all members of a society at various times use a restricted code. Yet, while some members acquire the use of an elaborated code and utilize language in a flexible fashion, fitting what they say to the demands of the situation, there are others who are wholly confined to using variants of a restricted code. It is their *only* form of speech. They have failed to select appropriate meanings and therefore their verbalizations are inadequate for formal communication. Furthermore, Bernstein says that such individuals will be found predominantly among the lower working class.

In his earliest writing Bernstein suggested that, for the working classes, their position in the social structure of our society was one in which there would be a particular emphasis on mechanical solidarity. His argument was of course a sociological one. More recently, however, he has become dissatisfied with the traditional economic and educational indices of social class. He has attempted rather to examine certain types of nuclear family in order to uncover the genesis of conditions which would lead to restricted code use. This typology of families might, of course, be strongly associated with social class as traditionally measured. Bernstein in his research has concentrated on aspects of child rearing which might be crucial for the full development of language. An example of this was an enquiry into the amount a mother reports talking to her child and what sort of occasions she is likely to see as relevant for conversation with him. In general he has been concerned to examine the mother's emphasis upon and contextual use of language. From these studies there emerged differences between mothers in the use of language in the socialization of children. In these ways Bernstein is attempting to isolate common features in the type, amount and range of communication within the different families. Thus he hopes eventually to establish a typology of families which would be based upon these common features and which would be associated with the emergence of a restricted language in the child. This work is fully described in a paper which has already been published in this series.[6]

This returns us to a point touched upon earlier. If an individual, for whatever reason, were confined to a restricted form of speech, what would be the consequences for him? We have already hinted at some general social disadvantagement as an obvious one, and, though we do not need to go into it again, it is for us perhaps the most important consequence. As Jesperson[7] has observed:

> It is to the advantage of the children to speak standard English not only materially, because they can more easily obtain positions in society which now—whether one approves it or not in the abstract—are given by preference to people whose speech is free of dialect, but also because they thus escape being looked down on on account of their speech, and are therefore saved from many unpleasant humiliations. Apart from all this merely by reason of their speaking they have a better chance of coming in contact with others and getting a fuller exchange of ideas.

However, there may be further aspects of this disadvantagement. We want to focus our attention now on another relationship, that of the linguistically disadvantaged child to the educational system, and to consider the effect of this disadvantagement on his general cognitive functioning. Bernstein has focused considerable attention on these two latter issues.

Bernstein is not alone in his attempt to spell out the functional relationship between language and thinking processes. A large area of psychology investigates this very problem. It is unfortunate that there is not the space here to describe some of the different types of approaches which have been taken up. It is important to distinguish Bernstein's thesis from the thesis of Benjamin Lee Whorf. Put in the most general form, the Whorfian theory asserts that the vocabulary and structure of a language determine the conception and thinking of the speakers. It means here that the categories we use to process our experience of the environment can only be those which exist in the language. Whorf[8] catalogued many differences between the various languages—not just differences in lexis, as one would find for example when comparing Dutch and German—but differences in terms of the meanings and ideas expressed in the language. To give a very simple example here, we might only have the words 'red' and 'yellow' and no such word as 'orange'. The theory asserts that in such a case our perception of colour falling mid-way between red and yellow would be rather different from the individual who had a main category for 'orange'. Or consider another example. We have one word 'aunt' which signifies four biologically distinct relationships: father's sister, mother's sister, father's brother's wife, and mother's brother's wife. However, languages all over the world group these relationships in distinct ways.[9] For example, one language has a term for all the female relatives of the mother's family, and another term for all the female relatives of the father's family. These terms may, and in some cases do, indicate different types of relationship requiring different attitudes and behaviours. Another language will not have verb forms indicating differences in tense, but only of degree of certainty of the action referred to.

Many of the differences described by Whorf reflect in some sense the relevance or criticality of the phenomena. For example, in one area of the Philippine Islands, where rice is a staple diet, and therefore, a daily occurrence, and where such familiarity leads to the detection of small differences between rices, there are 92 *named* varieties of rice.[10] In England we have one word 'rice', although we make distinctions between different sorts using rather cumbersome phraseology like 'long grained rice' or purely borrowed phraseology such as 'Uncle Ben's Rice'. The Filipino child, in learning his language, learns both the names and distinctive features of the 92 varieties.

It is a very complex matter to *demonstrate* that particular sets of linguistic categories are responsible for widely varying perceptual experiences and modes of thinking. Nevertheless, evidence exists that there is indeed a relationship between the linguistic categories that we have available and the non-linguistic categories that we use.

Bernstein's thesis is different from that of Whorf: Bernstein maintains that a whole range of speech codes can arise *within* a common language. He sees the culture acting selectively upon the development of speech codes and the social structure as determining their usage. Caution is needed here. For example, we have suggested that the degree of relevance or criticality of an experience determines the finesse of the discrimination we make. A coalminer may have a restricted language with respect to all areas of experience except coal, where he probably makes such discriminations that it would take the rest of us months to learn and for which he has a rich technical vocabulary. This coalminer might have a number of terms for coal not found in the language generally, that is, his vocabulary in this area is an extended one. Nevertheless, his use of these terms in the structure of his speech generally would coincide with what we believe to be the features of restricted code. The restricted code user operates with a smaller range of fine linguistic distinctions than the elaborated code user, except perhaps with respect to particular circumscribed areas. If we return to our example from earlier on, our imaginary hippies, we note that restricted code appears to have a different function from elaborated code. For one thing, the speaker is not impelled to give a very precise meaning to what he says; a very general one will do, so long as it fits in with what the others are expecting and does not divide the group's sense of cohesion by generating questions, expressions of disbelief or objection. It is a general atmosphere of concordance which is relevant and critical to the restricted code user. The subtleties of meaning, the intentions and private experience of the individual, do not find their way into the vocabulary of the restricted code user. For example, in Bernstein's theory, emotion and its expression are singled out for attention. One of the most distinctive characteristics of emotion is its private nature. Experience, say of jealousy, has its unique component which can be communicated only with difficulty by individuals eager to communicate it in situations with ready listeners. An individual engulfed in a group process is unlikely to ever encounter conditions in which his unique experience of jealousy is relevant for verbal contribution. How can he and why should he analyse its distinctive flavour? Where and when would he have acquired the words with which to communicate it? Together with emotion stands the communication of experience of ourselves, of our relationships with others, of relationships between others; all these are likely to suffer the same fate as private emotion. Like the 91 other varieties of rice, the subtleties of private emotion may be *felt* but not raised to a level of specific verbal meanings.

Restricted code is initiated in a social context and initially has its social function. Language for a restricted code user is not a medium for exploring logic or relative truth in argument, nor for weighing opinion. It is tied to its context and in a sense loses its uniquely abstract quality. A pre-school child's tentative explorations of the distinction between 'you need not' and 'you must not' is relevant and important in one family setting but passes without comment in another. His table-time remark that his drink was pink and now is red is not relevant: drinks are only to be rapidly drunk with the minimum of mess. His emerging observation that Uncle Henry is nice but quiet and Uncle Jack is noisy and funny is lost beneath a general prescription as to how he should behave in the presence of all older male relatives. It is not so much a question of the presence or absence of a feature of language, i.e. adjectives, passive verbs, but rather of which aspects of reality are made relevant for explicit and individuated verbalization.

Unlike Whorf, Bernstein cannot as yet point to specific features of restricted code and show how these produce specific failures of discrimination or categorization. He is suggesting something rather general. If an individual does not have a language with refined categories and varying vocabulary to reflect the fine discriminations and infinitely varying experiences that his perceptual and sensory system could make available to him, then he is going to miss out on them. If he has never used language as a system for tracing out some logical relationships or manipulating and comparing ideas, that is, if he has not used the most abstract function of language, then how does he perform these operations when required to in the formal education system? If this kind of abstract behaviour has never been relevant *for speech*, it can never *in fact* have been relevant. It would be hardly surprising if such individuals showed signs of atrophy when performing on intelligence tests. Nor would it be surprising if the educational system with an emphasis on knowledge and activities for their own sakes and on far distant goals should make less impact on the restricted code user.

The child entering school at five years, these days, is seen as a potential intellectual with a passion for discovery. Which he is. He is seen as possessing a brain and a nervous system capable of processing rather complex data. Which it does! For some children, however, this will be the first time they have been viewed in this light. Consider a five-year-old boy whose parents are both teachers. His parents will have observed his pleasure in making logical distinctions, or symmetrical patterns, or perhaps simply his musical ability and disinterest in reading. They will have already noted in considerable detail his clearly intellectual performances. They will have made available by conversation and by provision of carefully designed toys and so on an opportunity for him to develop his intellectual ability. And they will be in a degree of concordance about his interests. Consider on the other hand a five-year-old boy whose mother is a housewife and whose father is a docker in a dockers' community. There are certain features of this child which will dominate all other features in terms of relevance. Firstly that he is a boy rather than a girl will be impressed on him far more frequently and vividly than that he has mechanical ability rather than artistic ability. That his father is a docker and does a man's job, a job his mother could not do even if she wanted to, will also be impressed upon him. The point here is that the relevant aspects of his life are rather sociological. The emphasis is on his role in a system where groups and norms are important.

The innate intelligence of these two children may be remarkably similar, although manifested in quite different ways. The degree to which they are attuned to the requirements and opportunities of school life are already widely different. For the former, school is simply an extension (with better equipment) of the life he leads at home. For the latter, whether it is interesting and exciting or not, it is a different world, and probably quite soon he comes to view it as a less real world. What is the medium through which these two world views show themselves? Simply the way in which language is used. When the teacher says 'Let's think of a word which means the same as shiny', she is asking the child to carry out a task which restricted code is never required to do. Such refinement of meaning is simply not necessary. When she says 'No, Charlie, the hamster died because of the lump on his head, he didn't get a lump on his head because he died', she is illustrating the vital function of a word, 'because', which for some children has always been embedded in some command like 'because-I-say-so'. For the child of restricted language something quite new is happening in the communication system, and he is already at a disadvantage compared with the child for whom such language is not new. A child must learn that sentences are made of separate words which can be changed or rearranged. Also that such substitution and rearrangements are very important for conveying differences in meaning. Yet hitherto his experience may have been limited to invariant inevitable sequences like 'wipeyerfeetorI'lltellyerdad'. He will only have been dimly aware of words as separate entities. Written language is at a further stage of abstraction than spoken language, that is, for the restricted code user even further removed from his normal use and experience of language. If the restricted code child's perception of language is already somewhat inappropriate for certain contexts, he must suffer from handicaps in achieving basic literacy. Later on in English lessons, demands will be made upon him to use language flexibly for a large number of different purposes, all of which require his arranging words and structures appropriately, making subtle substitutions to fit precise meanings. He is asked for orginality in his style and expression. Coherence is necessary in most of the information he will have to process and record. For many of us, this degree of literacy makes no more demand on us than has been made on our speech from a very early age. For others, however, it is almost like achieving literacy in a foreign language. We can hardly be surprised if this level of achievement is generally not high.

How much does a sound language system facilitate the mastery of scientific and mathematical skills? This question is a difficult, technical and controversial one. We do not know whether some kinds of concepts are acquired non-verbally. Nor do we know the *exact* role of words on the acquisition of those concepts which *are* acquired verbally. We have already drawn attention to the fact that a great deal of psychological work is carried out in this area; some psychologists are interested in how the verbal experience of children affects their verbal learning—their ability to remember words and sequences of words. Others are interested in how verbal cues are used in learning concepts and in using them. Yet others, in the role that verbal formulation plays in solving problems of various types. We cannot go into these problems here. In evaluating our project we explored certain tasks in which the children had to use verbal cues and found some very interesting results. These will be discussed in a later section.

In his early papers Bernstein stated a number of cognitive deficiencies or differences which would follow on habitual restricted code use. The relationship which he has proposed has yet to be proved. For one thing, as we have shown, the restricted code child is disadvantaged in school anyway—we do not know whether intellectual deficiencies are consequential purely upon language or upon a multitude of interacting factors, with language as one of them. However, Bernstein has concerned himself with intelligence test performances and social class. He has shown, for example, that on those parts of intelligence tests which tap verbal ability, working-class children (or potential restricted code adults) perform at an inferior level. He has also shown that with individuals from lower and upper social classes matched on non-verbal I.Q. scores, the higher the non-verbal score for the working class subject, the greater the discrepancy between verbal and non-verbal scores. He argues that the non-verbal score is some index of innate endowment, and the discrepancy indicates the degree to which an intelligent working-class subject is hindered by his inadequate verbal system.

We might summarize at this point the consequences of confinement to a restricted form of speech. There is the spiral of underachievement starting early in school; there are enormous social disadvantages; also we suggest tentatively that there may be a concurrent perceptual illiteracy and insensitivity to certain varieties of experience; there may be failures in conceptualization and abstraction due to inappropriate language functioning.

We now come to the main theme of this book. What can be done educationally for the child handicapped by having only a restricted form of speech?

In the United States the general problem of culturally deprived children and their educational performance has been tackled on a wide scale with pre-school programmes. Some of these programmes focus particularly on language, but not all. The problem, for example, of the negro urban slum child is more dramatic and also more general than the problem we are interested in here. The programmes which have been carried out have usually taken the form of extra nursery school education from the age of three until compulsory education begins. These special schools simply aim to give children the type of nursery school education which middle-class children often have anyway. Some of them more ambitiously link these projects with schemes aimed at also helping the parents of the children. They attempt to compensate for the many deprivations such children suffer. One programme at least has attempted to provide an intensive language training programme on a formal academic basis. All these programmes, however, are designed to be carried out under special conditions; that is, buildings, equipment and teachers are all recruited for the purpose. Our project was of a different nature. We aimed to produce a programme which any teacher with a standard training could use in the ordinary classroom. We aimed to teach children to use a language both formal and flexible—the one through which education is mediated—the only one in which expression can fit individual experience and needs. An analogy suggests itself here. In Switzerland all members of the population speak a language dialect called Swiss-German. This varies from area to area. It has a few features in common with High German. In schools most children learn to speak High German, the formal written language of the country. Now probably this German dialect is not comparable to restricted code in its paucity. The point, however, is that most young Swiss regardless of class or intelligence acquire a formal language, High German, which they can use when the occasion demands, using the dialect for more local settings. We would argue that the restricted code user is in a somewhat similar position to the Swiss. He has a language which serves mainly social and local purposes well and appropriately; it is essentially a spoken language. Yet he must, if he is to extend his world beyond the purely local, learn another language different in function and more difficult. There is no reason why most members of the population in the United Kingdom should not learn their 'High' English too; for whatever other reasons educational bias might work against the lower-class child, language would not be one of them. In fact, a successful campaign to equip all children with adequate spoken language might be one of the greatest blows against a class system which has changed less than we often like to believe.

Our aim, then, was to elaborate and broaden the spoken language of children whom we believed would otherwise suffer from the disadvantages we have described. We wanted to do this with children right from the beginning of compulsory education, so that the basis on which their essential literacy depends would have been improved from the onset. The next chapter describes how the project was set up, the area and schools chosen, and how plans for evolving a programme together with the teachers were worked out.

Chapter 2   On the Site

Two considerations determined the form that our project was to take. Firstly, we wanted to set up a programme which would explore the possibilities of extending the spoken language of young children and yet could be carried out by teachers with no special training and with a limited amount of new materials. It should be readily adjustable to any classroom by any normally trained teacher. Secondly, we wanted to intervene as early as possible in the children's educational career and to maximize on the handicaps, actual and potential, that they might have. They should be taken from that section of the school population seen as having the poorest prognosis for their school life.

If we were to ask a teacher or educationalist to predict what classes of children at age five would produce a high percentage of early drop-outs from the educational system at fifteen, he would almost certainly include any class of five year olds coming from a predominantly working-class area, with a fair sprinkling of immigrant children speaking largely incomprehensible English or in some cases no English at all. In addition, these children would be scheduled for only two years in the infant school and would enter the junior school along with children who would have had two full terms more than they had had in the infant school. Thus, apart from the linguistic handicaps that they might be assumed to have by reason of their working-class background, they would be further penalized from the onset of their school career simply by being born in the wrong part of the year. Should any of these children eventually arrive in the grammar school or the upper streams of the comprehensive school they would be more the exception than the rule. For an educational research project this class of children presents the greatest challenge, and accordingly we decided to work with such a group. This chapter will be concerned with a description of the children in our sample and the factors determining their selection.

Area

Our research project was carried out in an East London Borough which consists almost entirely of working and lower working classes, and with a considerable influx of immigrants from the West Indies, Pakistan and India during the lifetime of the project. In a report which he published shortly before the onset of the project, the educational psychologist of the area stated that there seemed to be a general exodus of 'bright children' from the Borough and that the social class categories of the population were almost certainly becoming progressively lower. People in the higher ranges of the working classes were tending to move out of the Borough. However, at the onset of the project, when the sample of the children was selected, this exodus was no more than a steady trickle and was not, we believe, responsible for the rather atypical educational record of the Borough.

We did not choose this Borough simply because of its fairly homogeneous working-class population, but because its educational record was of particular interest. The problem in working-class areas is often confounded by old and ill-equipped buildings, but in this Borough the L.E.A. was noticeable for its most generous provision of up-to-date equipment and materials and for its efforts to bring even its oldest Victorian buildings up to the standard of post-war schools. Yet the evidence from the 11 + selection and from the record of passes in the G.C.E. for the five years previous to the onset of the project revealed serious problems. Comparing the distribution of I.Q.s obtained in the 11 + selection with those collected for the national average population, it was found that the Borough consistently returned about 5·5% of children at an I.Q. level of 119 and above instead of the 10% that would be predicted in terms of the national average. Whereas at the bottom of the I.Q. distribution the Borough returned about twice as many as would be predicted. This pattern was consistent for both intelligence and achievement. In other words, the 11 + selection tests revealed a consistent pattern of intelligence and attainment in which the top ranges of both were depleted and the lower ranges were excessive. This meant that the L.E.A. had difficulty in filling its selective (grammar) schools. The 'cut-off' point for automatic transfer to a selective school was at an I.Q. of about 107, some eight to ten points below the cut-off adopted in most areas in the country.*

Analysis of the G.C.E. results for the Borough, that is the success

---

* We were indebted to A. T. Ravenette for this information.

rate of children who had had selective education after passing the 11+, also revealed a problem. The success gradient ran from 42% in English through 51% in Mathematics to 75% in Natural Sciences. There seemed to be then a differential pattern of educational attainment even amongst the brighter children in the Borough, which suggested a differential pattern of intellectual abilities.

A. T. Ravenette,[11] as a result of these findings, examined the pattern of abilities of a large group of secondary school children in the Borough. The age range was from twelve to fifteen. He found that, using standardized tests of intelligence, the verbal ability of these children was significantly lower than their non-verbal ability, and this was especially so at the highest levels of non-verbal ability. There was a dearth of children with high verbal scores on the test. Also, within the age range investigated there was a relative deterioration in ability with increasing age, and this was greater for verbal ability.

Here then was a Borough, which, despite the outstanding efforts of its L.E.A. to provide the best educational facilities for its children, revealed both in its educational record each year and in the results of independent educational research, a picture which Bernstein's theory of restricted code seemed to fit exactly. We were presented with a population of children possessing a differential pattern of intellectual abilities and who were increasingly handicapped as they moved through their school careers and by the possession of a restricted language.

Schools

There were thirty-seven primary schools in the Borough. An increasingly large number were of post-war construction and, as we have already mentioned, all were generously equipped with up-to-date materials and equipment. Nine of these thirty-seven schools took part in the project. In order to ensure that any differences that we observed at the end of the project could be attributed to the project itself and not to already existing differences between schools, the selection of schools was determined on the basis of several criteria. Firstly, all nine schools were non-denominational. Secondly, the infant and junior sections of each school had separate head teachers. Thirdly, they were all housed in old buildings at least 50 years old. Fourthly, schools with nursery feeders were excluded. Fifthly, and most importantly, the average I.Q. based on 11+ selection tests at the end of the Junior School for the previous four years was roughly comparable.

The nine schools selected were then divided into three groups of three. The first group of three acted as experimental schools (hereafter to be referred to as E1 schools) in which a language training programme was carried out. The second group of three schools (designated C1) acted as pure controls in so far as they were only used for before and after measurements. The final group of three schools (designated C2) also acted as a control group, but of a different kind.

A major difficulty which arises in educational research is the effect that conducting a research project has on the motivation of the teachers. It is possible to conduct a training programme in schools, obtain clear differences at the end in performance between the experimental and control groups and yet be unable to determine whether the observed differences are due to the training procedure itself (new techniques, methods, equipment, timetable, classroom organization, etc.) or to a general increase in the teacher's motivation which has benefited the children. Simply taking part in a research project may so affect the teacher that she becomes more energetic and enthusiastic to have her pupils shine. The history of educational research is scattered with examples of research projects, large- and small-scale experiments, that have demonstrated the 'effect' of some experimental intervention on the children, but in which the teacher's motivation is not taken into account. Thus, if and when the supposedly 'improved' techniques, skills, organization or what have you are more widely adopted, the disappointment that results in not finding the effects repeated is not surprising.

Although it is extremely difficult to control for, let alone measure, this effect on the outcome of a research project, we attempted a partial solution to the problem by including this third group of C2 schools in the design. We will describe the way in which we used these schools in a later section. It only needs to be pointed out at this stage that the teachers in the C2 schools were very much part of the research project but, to the best of our knowledge, had no part in or awareness of the language training programme taking place in the three E1 schools.

So then, we had three groups of three schools, all having the same kind of internal organizational structure and all occupying the same kind of building with the same kinds of facilities. Assigning these schools to the three groups was determined by two factors: firstly, comparability of intelligence test results at the end of the junior school, the three schools showing the highest average I.Q. being assigned one to each group; and secondly, on the basis of comparability in catchment area. Since there were probably social class differences within the Borough (for example, the northern part is regarded by the inhabitants of the Borough as the smarter part), we also assigned schools from each catchment area of the Borough one to each group. It should be pointed out, however, that by starting with only thirty-seven schools and operating with a number of criteria to arrive at the threefold division of nine schools we have described, the matching of schools was at best only a rough one. There was also, of course, no guarantee that the I.Q. picture for the previous four years at the junior level was being maintained at the infant level. In fact, when the ability of the children selected to take part in the project was measured at the onset of the project, we found the distribution of ability across the three groups of schools (E1, C1 and C2) to be slightly biased in favour of E1.

Children

Since we believed that the particular linguistic handicaps associated with membership of the working class are operative from the earliest years, we decided to intervene as early as possible in the school life of the children. We ruled out nursery school intervention largely on the grounds that within a working-class area having only limited nursery school facilities, we would be likely to encounter a biased sample of children, when what we wanted was a sample that could be considered as truly representative of the local population. Consequently, we chose to run a training programme for the duration of the first three years of compulsory schooling, that is, from the moment of the child's first direct contact with educational agencies in the reception class of the infant school through to the end of the first year in junior school. Research funds limited the total lifetime of the project to three years.

Our sample of children consisted of all children born between April and September, 1959, who entered the nine infant schools during the autumn term of 1964. These children were to have only two years in the infant school before moving on to junior school. This gave us initially 231 children, 113 boys and 118 girls. It included sixteen West Indians and one Nigerian. Since most of these West Indians were recent arrivals to the United Kingdom and had not shared the common background of the rest of the sample, we did not include them or the Nigerian in any analysis. Intelligence tests and speech samples taken during the three years of the project indicated that this sub-sample of West Indians constituted a special problem—somewhat akin to that found with Puerto Rican immigrants and Negro immigrants from the South in the larger northern cities of the United States. We believe that the methods and techniques that we developed during the lifetime of the project are equally applicable to immigrant children and, in fact, many ideas were formulated as a result of the problems which arose in the class which centred on these children. This reduced the initial sample to 214 children. A further five children were also excluded, as we were not able to obtain any baseline measures of their intelligence or linguistic ability. Two of them were retained subsequently in the infant school at the end of the two years and were later transferred to an E.S.N. school. We began the project then with a final sample of 209 children, 99 boys and 110 girls. Table 1 in Appendix 1 shows the number of children in each of the three groups of schools.

During the first term the classes in the nine schools consisted only of children from our sample. In the spring and summer terms they were joined by children who were to have two years and two terms in the infant school, that is, children who remained in the infant school for a third year. The training programme did not commence until the beginning of the spring term when the average size of the class was 35. All the children in the classes, both sample and non-sample children, took part in all activities. There was no discrimination of sample children from non-sample children in the training activities, only in evaluation and measurement by visiting researchers; and even this was largely disguised from the children by having all children in the class seen by the visitor. The teachers in *all* nine schools knew who the sample children were in their classes.

A major problem arising in any long-term research project is the loss of sample children through transfer to other schools. During the three years of our research we lost nearly a quarter (22·5%) of our sample, 23·2% of the boys and 21·8% of the girls. Of the 209 children in the sample at the beginning, only 162 remained at the end. Most of the drop-outs were in fact moves out of the Borough. Table 2 in Appendix 1 shows the number of children left in each of the three groups of schools after three years.

This shrinkage of the sample raised an important question for the research. We have already referred to the area psychologist's report that there was a general exodus of 'bright' children from the Borough. Did this mean then that the sample of children we ended up with was less bright than the sample we started with? Some time during the fourth, fifth and sixth weeks of their first term in the reception class, all the children in the sample were given a battery of intelligence tests and a structured interview in which their speech was recorded for later analysis. The administration of the intelligence tests and the collection of samples of speech were carried out by different researchers on separate occasions. The three intelligence tests given were Raven's Coloured Progressive Matrices[12] which is a non-verbal test of intelligence, the Crichton Vocabulary Scale[13] which is a test of active vocabulary in which the child has to provide word definitions, and the English Picture Vocabulary Scale[14] which is a test of word recognition in which the child indicates to which of four pictures a word refers. We shall refer to this test as the E.P.V.T.

The reasons for giving these tests were several. Firstly, we wanted to make sure that our division of schools into three groups had not produced any bias in ability. Secondly, we needed a baseline of ability against which to measure any improvement during the project. Finally, we wanted to make a comparison with a group of middle-class children to determine whether there were class differences at age five and if so, whether they were similar to those observed by Bernstein with adolescents which we have described in the first chapter.

The results, which are to be found in Tables 3, 4 and 5 in Appendix 1, were rather surprising. Firstly, whilst there was no difference between the groups on the Matrices non-verbal test, there was a difference in favour of E1 group on both tests of verbal ability. Though this difference was not significant for the E.P.V.T. it was significant beyond the ·01 level for the Crichton. Thus, in spite of the precautions we had taken in assigning schools to the three groups, we were presented with a definite bias in our favour. This meant that the evaluation of the language programme was made more difficult than it would have been had the groups been comparable at the onset. Consequently, much of the evaluation we shall describe had to be carried out on subsamples matched on ability as measured by the verbal tests at the beginning of the project.

Secondly, there was a sex difference in verbal ability. On both the Crichton Vocabulary Scale and the E.P.V.T. boys produced a significantly higher mean score than the girls. For the E.P.V.T. this was not too surprising, as several investigators have reported that boys tend to do better than girls on tests of word recognition. Nevertheless, the sex difference found during the standardization of the E.P.V.T. was not great enough to warrant separate norms for boys and girls. For the Crichton Vocabulary Scale the results were quite unexpected and just the reverse of what is usually reported. Girls almost invariably do better on vocabulary tests than boys. As we had available data on a group of 148 children of the same age randomly sampled from five schools in a solidly middle-class area in South-East London, we were able to make a number of comparisons and, in particular, to see whether the atypical sex difference in verbal ability found in our working-class sample also held for middle-class children of the same age. On all three tests the middle-class children obtained higher mean scores than the working-class children, but there were no significant sex differences. The means on the verbal tests were slightly higher for the boys, but not significantly so. Table 6, Appendix 1, shows the results obtained by the middle-class children on all three tests.

A third finding was that, though the working-class children did not obtain as high a mean score as the middle-class children, nevertheless the scores were unexpectedly high, especially on the verbal tests. Since Raven's Matrices only provides normative data from age $5\frac{1}{2}$ years onwards, we were not able to make a direct comparison of our slightly younger sample of children with the general population. However, since the mean raw score on the Matrices for the general population at age $5\frac{1}{2}$ years is 14, and our sample of working-class children obtained a mean raw score of 13, it seems likely that our sample was typical of the general population. On the other hand, the mean raw score of 14·87 obtained by the 148 middle-class children probably indicates a group of children of superior non-verbal ability. Normative data on the Crichton Vocabulary Scale is provided from $4\frac{1}{2}$ years onward at half-yearly intervals and, though the population upon which the test was standardized was rather small, we were able to make a direct comparison. The median raw score at age 5 for the Crichton standardization population is 13, which is some 3 points lower than the 16·02 obtained by our working-class sample and some 5 points lower than the mean score of 18·08 obtained by the middle-class sample. However, if we take into account the small size of the standardization population and the fact that the working-class mean of 16·02 is equivalent to the median raw score of this population at age $5\frac{1}{2}$, the result is less startling than it appears at first. However, when we turn to the second of the two verbal tests, the E.P.V.T., we cannot question the standardization data. The test was standardized on 867 children aged between $5-0$ and $5-11$ and provides norms at monthly intervals. Raw scores are transformed into standardized scores having a mean of 100 and a standard deviation of 15. Our working-class sample obtained a mean standardized score of 101·02 (103·14 for the boys and 99·12 for the girls) and the middle-class sample obtained a mean of 110·43 (110·87 for the boys and 109·95 for the girls). Whilst the most striking feature of these results was the very large class difference, we also found that the working-class group obtained a mean score 1 point above the mean for the population at large.

To summarize the results then, we found ourselves with a sample of 5 year old working-class children whose verbal and non-verbal ability was distributed in the same way as that of the general population. And although their performance was already at age 5 inferior to that of the middle-class children, it was much better than that which is invariably found with older children of the same class. The results then supported our contention that the working-class child at 5 has a potential which he progressively fails to realize as he passes up through the school. They strengthened our belief that, if the social class gap was to be prevented from growing any wider, some form of additional training was badly needed in working-class schools from the beginning of the child's school career. Since we regarded the differential development of language skills between social classes as the major factor responsible for the increasingly different levels of performance of children of different social classes as they move up through the school, the specific aim of our project was to explore the possibilities of providing additional training in language skills.

We began this discussion of the intelligence characteristics of the children when considering the problem of sample shrinkage. Compared with the total sample of 209 children the 47 drop-outs did not differ appreciably in their mean score on any of the three ability tests, but at the level of experimental group there was a definite tendency for *brighter* children to have dropped out of E1 and for duller children to have left C1 and C2. The constantly changing size of the sample during the three years of the project together with the differential drop-out from the three groups raised certain problems for evaluation which we shall discuss in Chapter 6.

We have already mentioned that in addition to the tests of verbal and non-verbal intelligence given at the onset of the project, we also collected samples of speech from each child during a structured interview. However, we were not able to use this data to assess the initial comparability of E1, C1 and C2 children. The kind of analysis which has been developed by the linguists in the Research Unit over the past four years and which is still being refined was not available during the lifetime of the project. Nor does it yield simple numerical values to indicate a child's position on a scale of linguistic maturity. We shall discuss the difficulties and problems involved in assessing linguistic maturity on the basis of recorded speech samples in the later chapter on evaluation. We need only point out at this stage that for all purposes of evaluation the initial comparability of groups and sub-groups within the sample was always based on performance on the tests of verbal ability.

Chapter 3   Questions and Questions

Our aim in the project was in a way two-fold. We wanted to produce a language programme for daily use in the classroom. More generally, we also wanted to orient the teachers towards the opportunities for using and improving the children's speech during many activities throughout the school day. It is this latter aspect which we shall discuss first. Basically, we intended using situations which occur continually during the school day and activities and lessons which are common to most infant and junior schools. Children, if given the opportunity, talk a great deal to each other and to the teacher, during most activities. This is a source of difficulty, since most classrooms are somewhat overcrowded and the noise level which is reached by unprohibited child talk does very little to further education. Nevertheless, we feel that teachers who are aware of the importance of coherent and flexible speech will turn to good account a feature of children's behaviour which is often a nuisance. Left to themselves, children talk about their classroom activities both to each other and to the teacher in a manner which is often abbreviated or incoherent or inadequate, or all three. Clearly it is impossible to carry on formal corrective conversation with forty children simultaneously. We suggest, however, the following as examples of situations where the teacher is often alone with a small group of children, and which would provide an ideal context for the kind of conversation we have in mind.

Curiosity, Questions and Explanations

In Chapter 1 we suggested that the child who has a restricted language will have acquired it in an environment where language is seen as having rather limited functions. His tentative comments at home about the colour of the potatoes or the liquid in his cup, his questions about the working of the drainage system, or why

26

Uncle Charlie hasn't been around for some time, are unlikely to be taken up, improved upon and answered, or even noticed. They are more likely to be engulfed in a number of prescriptions for immediate behaviour on his part and not seen as occasions for developing knowledge or language skill. It is for these kinds of reasons that the child's language becomes restricted in use and style.

In schools there are probably as many occasions for comment and questioning as at home. The environment is already a lively and a stimulating one. Children's spontaneous questions and comments provide tremendous opportunities for discussion in which the teacher by example and probing can show what constitutes adequate answers and precisely phrased questions. For example, one good strategy often consists of (a) phrasing her answer in such a way that it evokes a further, possibly better, more precise question, and (b) sometimes referring the child's question back to him. Here is an example. The teacher might bring into the classroom an old clock with the mechanism exposed and without comment start to examine it, perhaps to try to wind it. Among a small group it might evoke such questions as 'What is that?', 'What are you doing that for?', etc. The teacher might reply 'Don't you recognize it?' or 'Is there something wrong with it?' and so on. Of course, teachers have to be looking out for such props for these sorts of occasions, but a range of items will serve equally well as the old clock; for example, hour glasses, caterpillars, pomegranates, unusual photographs or pictures, and so forth. The point here is that the element of spontaneity and unpredictability, together with the lack of premature comment on the teacher's part, is sufficient to evoke the comments and questions she is hoping for. Teachers frequently introduce new visual aids into the classroom anyway. These are not often as fully utilized as they might be, possibly because classrooms tend to have a bit too much on the walls, and the children stop looking at them. When a teacher puts up on the wall a new picture, chart, frieze or whatever, she should choose her moment, when the children are fairly quiet and not too busy with anything else. If, without comment, she puts up some interesting new item, again children are likely to comment and question spontaneously. If it is there on the wall already when they enter the classroom in the morning, most of their comments and questions will be lost among themselves and the teacher will have lost her chance.

In fact, the teacher does not always have to provide the occasions and materials herself. Almost any day, children, particularly boys, will bring some object, piece of equipment, toy or novelty, whose purpose is not immediately apparent. Teachers should be on the look-out for this. The teacher can, without comment, during a moment when the children are attentive but not too busy, invite the child to hold up the article. Again this invokes a mixture of questions, comments and answers, unfortunately often simultaneous. She can select questions and comments for the kind of treatment we have already described. She can make frequent use of probes, such as, 'What do you mean?' or 'What do you think Tony means, children?' By employing these kinds of strategies she is illustrating what are apt questions and, more importantly, what are adequate answers.

During the school day many extraneous events occur which teachers often regard as rather a nuisance and about which questions tend to be suppressed as trivial. Yet they can be turned to good account. For example, it happens rather often that a child arrives late or leaves during a lesson with his mother. The purpose is often medical. The children usually want to know what is going on. They ask each other about it. Again the teacher can take up these questions and comments and invite a child who happens to know what is happening to explain to the rest of the class. Similar use can be made of such events as visits by workmen, inspectors, strangers and so on. The general aim is to have children questioning their environment at every level, to reinforce their curiosity and to improve upon and elaborate on the form these questions and comments take.

News Time

News time is a feature of most infant and some junior schools. It consists of one or two children telling the class about events of interest which have occurred to them personally. It is successful or not depending on the interest of the material the child has available and on his eloquence in narrating it. It will be seen in the next chapter that we also used News Time in our twenty minutes' daily programme. In a sense, however, it is an activity which is more successful the more spontaneously it occurs. Again the teacher can be watchful for events which children can tell to the class, for sessions lasting not more than a few minutes or so. For example, children go out to the playground three times during the day. While they are there, it sometimes happens that they evolve a particularly exciting and imaginative game in which several members of the class are involved. The teacher can occasionally, not regularly, after the children have come in and settled down, issue the following invitation, 'Who has had a good game out in the playground?' She must then take care to exclude such games which are rather technical like football, and then invite the participants to stand up and spend a couple of minutes telling the class what they did. Again she can use prompts and probes of the sort we have already described.

Sometimes a child is sent with a message to another classroom. On his return the teacher can ask him to describe to the class what he thought was happening in the other classroom. This won't always evoke interesting material, but it will occasionally.

A child who is away for a long period, perhaps even in hospital, can also describe his experiences and answer questions put to him by the others.

The point here is that the teacher has an opportunity to intervene, correct and elaborate upon the children's efforts by asking questions and by asking for more precise descriptions and explanations. With co-operative effort other children can fill in where one has failed to make himself clear or has left out important or interesting items. Such co-operative efforts are particularly useful in that they demand attention from all the participants to the contribution of each member in order to give a good account.

Children can also be asked to find out things. They can be asked to find out how to make tea; how to mend a puncture; what kind of wall-paper they have in their sitting room; how their father mends a fuse; where the water supply comes from in the house; at what stage of completion an unfinished block of flats across the road is; how the builders started. Of course, children asked to find out such information frequently forget. They need to be reminded every day before going home and asked early during the next day. The point again is that the child has to produce an adequate account which can frequently be corrected or corroborated by other children.

None of these ideas introduces novel elements into the classroom. They simply constitute suggestions as to how fairly small and trivial events of the school day can be utilized for improving the children's language skill.

We have discussed so far the use of largely unplanned events in the school day. However, it is possible to exploit curriculum activities in a similar way. Later in school life children are asked to record in writing much of the practical work that they have done in geography, history, science and so on. In the early years children have available a shop, a nature table, a wendy house and other centres of interest. They engage in joint projects; they carry out small experiments. Until they can write, such activities are not verbally recorded or described, although they are sometimes drawn and painted. Yet in a sense their ability to make such recordings later must depend on their skill in talking about them now. We suggest, as in the previous section, that individual groups of children give accounts of projects which they have completed, both large and small. This is much more vivid and much more useful if these small accounts are conducted before an audience which has not been present. For example, teachers can occasionally 'borrow' each other, or the head mistress, or the lady who makes the tea and helps with the milk, or any other willing but ignorant listener. To ask children to tell each other or the teacher things which they already know about simply invites inadequate accounts, because detailed and explicit ones are not necessary and the children know that they are not. Another extremely useful aid here is a tape-recorder. In our programme, which is described in the following chapters, we in fact provided this as part of the equipment. Some schools have them already. If a tape-recorder is available, children can, with a little practice, produce accounts which they can record for the benefit of others in the school, for parents at open day, for visits, and so on. Later on, as well, such accounts can form the basis of written work which is part of basic skills.

Finally, we would like to suggest an emphasis which is often considered relatively unimportant, that of pronunciation and articulation. Thirty or forty years ago 'elocution' lessons used to be regarded as essential steps to genuine literacy, perhaps in some circles it still is so. Nowadays, however, in education we stress content rather than form and are reluctant to try to change the accent and grammatical faults of children. We shall not go into the virtues or insincerities of 'beautiful articulation' here. However, one feature that such training must have had was that of focusing attention on speech as an activity *per se*. A major difficulty with the child of restricted code is that his speech is no more than a sub-stratum against which his activities are carried out. He is no more aware of his speech or his intended words than he is of his breathing. We would suggest that teachers could draw attention to ambiguities and errors due to pronunciation as frequently, informally and humorously as possible, simply to get the children listening to themselves critically. To take an example, one teacher noticed that four words were used indistinguishably (from the point of view of pronunciation) by a number of children. The words were 'hill—eel—ill—heel', and they were all pronounced as 'eel'. Obviously in this case the meaning was carried by the context. We suggested that the next time one of these words occurred she might take time off for a few minutes for the following game:

Illustrate the meanings of the four words by drawings on the
blackboard. Then produce some sentences with the ubiquitous
'eel' making nonsense.

For example : Jack walked up the eel.
　　　　　　　The eel on my shoe is being mended.
　　　　　　　Susan was eel after the party.
　　　　　　　Joe found an eel in the pond.

Get the children to produce the correct pronunciation by
pretending not to understand them, until they are all making
the discrimination.

Many examples like this crop up, as do examples of ambiguity
due to grammatical errors. The teacher has to use tact about this
kind of correction. A child who is producing a (for him) very articu-
late thought-out story or description should not be cut off for a
lesson in elocution, which in any case is a job for the specialist.
The teacher may, indeed, prefer to set aside a time for talking,
when children know they are going to be listened to critically and
corrected. It is important that the children themselves criticize and
correct each other. In general, however, the teacher has to wait for
her opportunity and carry out the sequence informally rather than
dogmatically. Children quite possibly utilize their different speech as
a mark of group solidarity. They are reluctant to give up such a
symbol of it. Yet a teacher could stress that there are two languages
that the children speak—the language of inside the classroom and
the language of the playground. A small point here is that many
classrooms contain at least one child who speaks little or no English. Children are often very interested in this situation and in
the techniques of teaching the newcomer to speak English.
Such a child is an invaluable prop in our campaign. We can
stress the fact that little X is having to learn two languages. That
of his teacher inside the classroom and the language of his friends
at play in the playground. We can stress the differences ostensibly
for X's benefit. We can show the importance of articulation and
explicitness, again for X's benefit. We can make it a class project;
we hope without overwhelming X. We would stress that the major
aim of this activity is to try to get the children to take up a more
theoretical attitude towards their own speech.

All the activities we have suggested which involve descriptions
and narrations by individuals, and most of the activities in the
programme to be described, depend for their success on reasonable
articulation. One of the difficulties in the programme was that many
children were quite unable to speak loudly or clearly enough for
anyone else to hear or to understand them. This improves with age

and practice—it also improves with some training in articulation and a little healthy self-consciousness about speaking aloud.

In concluding this chapter it seems fair to point out that some infant school teachers are already oriented towards the opportunities for using and improving the speech of the children in their classes. For them the techniques and strategies we have described form an habitual part of their daily teaching style. But for the majority this is not the case. Whilst many teachers are all too aware of the glaring deficiencies in the verbal skills of their working-class pupils, they are not oriented towards dealing with these deficiencies except in the most formal manner. The approach that we adopted in our project was to regard the entire school day, from the moment the children entered the building, as a series of constantly changing opportunities for the teacher to explore the children's environment verbally with them. It is a skill that some teachers find hard to come by, and for them such an approach is at first a strain. To be continuously attentive to children's questions, to be always ready to build on the slightest remark and to provide the appropriate words, knowledge and interest, is a tall order, and especially so in a class of forty children. But we are convinced that such an approach is vitally important to the child's linguistic development and ultimately to his response to his school career. For these reasons we are convinced that such an approach must be adopted and maintained throughout the school day, no matter how slow the progress.

Chapter 4   Talk Reform

In an earlier chapter we discussed the nature of restricted code and the consequences for a child whose linguistic skills are confined to this mode of speech. In our language training programme we set up tasks for the children in which this type of speech would not be adequate. These tasks provided the context for the teacher attempting to increase the range of the lexis and structure. For it is not sufficient to require children to provide explanations, narrate stories, or give detailed descriptions, unless they are at the same time rapidly learning new words, new constructions, new expressions. On the other hand, formal teaching, as in academic approaches to second language learning, is dissonant with normal infant school teaching practice, and does not guarantee that children will utilize their knowledge in appropriate situations. The educationalists in the United States concerned with enrichment programmes are sharply divided on this issue. There are those who feel that intensive formal training is essential if linguistically deprived children are to catch up. Others feel that only the rich environment can generate a richer language. Thus we attempted to provide both components. The tasks and experiences which we asked the children to code, we have referred to as contexts; the activities purely designed to increase and correct the vocabularies and structures, we have called training, although the latter word rather distorts the actual game-like nature of these activities. A third element, which was also included in the programme, was aimed at the children's rather poor attention to and perception of speech generally. Both of these latter skills are prerequisites for more elaborate and refined use of language. There is also a certain amount of evidence that these skills are important for learning to read. Clearly any activities we introduced involved the need for attention, but we distinguished between those activities which were specifically training the children in purely attentional skills and those that were training the children in other skills.

33

We shall now present and describe all the activities used throughout the three year programme, then in the next chapter discuss the time tables and actual administration of these activities in our three experimental schools.

A   Activities for improving attention and auditory discrimination

(1)   The O'Grady game

(i)   Here we borrowed from the traditional children's party game and later elaborated on it. The children stand in a semi-circle around the teacher who follows the standard O'Grady format, e.g. 'O'Grady says: "Touch your nose." ' She accompanies each command with an appropriate gesture, e.g. she touches her own nose. Sometimes, however, she accompanies each command with an inappropriate gesture, e.g. she folds her arms. Thus the children have to attend only to her words while ignoring her gestures. When the game is thoroughly understood by all the children, the teacher introduces penalties when children respond incorrectly. Children who thus drop out are used as judges during the rest of the game. It usually takes some time before the average five-year-old child can suppress an action imitating what he sees in favour of one he hears.

(ii)   In this more difficult version the children must respond only to the 'O'Grady says . . .' trial and ignore both trials when the words 'O'Grady says' are omitted and trials when the teacher makes inappropriate gestures.

(iii)   Here the O'Grady instructions are aimed only at some of the children. The task is to decide for themselves whether they are eligible. For example, the teacher says 'O'Grady says: "put your hands over your ears if you have blue eyes".' Or 'O'Grady says: "stand on one leg those who can tell the time/know the date/feel hungry/are staying to lunch/ and so on".'

The O'Grady game did not last for more than ten minutes in any one session, and the stages proceeded as the children mastered each game. As will be seen from the timetable in the next chapter, O'Grady was discontinued and reintroduced at various points during the project.

(2)   Listening in the dark

The average infant school classroom is distracting as well as noisy. Quiet listening is very difficult to achieve. Early on in the project a special screened corner in the classrooms was set up where a tape-recorder and headphones were available. Here the children listened to stories. We soon observed that children found it difficult to sit and listen because of the movements in other parts of the class. This gave us the idea of making masks which the children could put on for specific listening tasks (usually lasting a very short time). The masks were of the fancy dress variety, purchased from a local joke shop and the eye holes blocked out with black adhesive tape. The children liked them enormously. Here are some of the listening games they played 'in the dark':

i   Recognizing voices

The children put on their personally selected masks. One child is selected and the teacher whispers a sentence to him which he then says aloud. The children must put up their hands to repeat the sentence and to name the child who had spoken it. She allows four or five guesses but no more before telling the children the name of the speaker. The activity is carried out very quickly and only four or five children have turns in any one session. The teacher keeps a record so that during a week all children have at least one turn. The activity involves the children in paying close attention both to the characteristics of voices as well as to what they say.

ii   Silly sentences

The teacher tells the children that when they have their masks on she is going to say something silly or something wrong. As soon as they hear it they must put up their hands to report it. A child who gets the answer right takes off his mask and watches the others. Sometimes the teacher says a sensible sentence (she informs the children of this). Here is an example of a silly sentence: 'John woke up very late the other morning. He got dressed. He put on his shoes, then he put on his socks and ran down stairs for breakfast'.

iii   Rhymes and poems

The children listen while the teacher recites a very short rhyme or poem. She repeats it twice. When she repeats it for the second time she stops at a particular point (having warned the children beforehand) and asks them for the next word or the next line or simply for what happens next. The children can respond in chorus or the teacher can select one child or she can alternate the two procedures.

iv 'What did I say?'

The teacher reads a short passage in which occur a number of nouns belonging to the same category. Initially she can tell the children what the category is. For example, it might be fruit. The children must listen carefully and then name an item which she has not yet mentioned. Later the children must decide for themselves what the category is, as well as producing a further example of it. Some teachers may prefer to introduce this game by using a list of nouns, only later graduating to the more difficult task of having the words embedded in a passage.

v Remembering in the dark

From time to time the teacher should draw the children's attention to a picture or poster or frieze in the classroom and should spend some time describing it and listing its elements. The next day the children put on their masks, and the teacher asks one of the children to describe the picture. The others must listen carefully and add details that are left out, correcting wrong descriptions. Another child then continues the description. The children are asked to think hard to remember the picture while the chosen child describes it.

vi The tape-recorder

Throughout the programme the children were provided with stories on tape. They listened to these in the screened corner using headphones attached to the tape-recorder. Some of this listening was purely passive, but occasionally they were asked to listen for specific items of information. To improve the quality and intensity of their listening the children (who always listened five at a time together) put on their masks to cut out visual distractions.

(3) Instruction chains

This is a game which can be played on a competitive basis using the class divided into groups. The task starts quite simply. The children carry out a few commands. Gradually, however, the number of commands to be remembered increases, and they are expressed in a syntactically complex way. Here is an example:

(a) Stand up.
   Walk to the door.
   Face the class.

(b) Stand up and walk to the door, then face the class.

(c) First stand up and then walk to the door, and *when you get there* face the class.

The teacher can increase the number of commands and the complexity of their expression separately or simultaneously. This will depend on how difficult the children find the task. The groups of children are awarded points for correct performance but also for correct criticism. (All the children must remember the instructions and monitor the individual's performance.)

(4) Telephones

The only unusual items of equipment that were used in the programme were simple battery-operated telephone circuits. Each class had two circuits, each consisting of two linked receivers. Three receivers were placed in the classroom and one elsewhere in the school. One was near the teacher's desk and was linked to another placed in the Wendy house. A light on the front of the receiver went on when the connected receiver was lifted off the hook.

The children arranged to work in pairs. They were given little boxes inside which were samples of material. These samples were of different colours, patterns and textures. The two children each had boxes containing an identical selection of samples. One child who could not be seen by his partner chose a piece in the box and described it carefully over the telephone. His partner had to choose the matching piece on the basis of this description. He, in turn, then chose another piece and instructed his partner. The two children would then meet at the teacher's desk to compare the samples chosen. Whilst, in fact, this activity demanded a number of skills, it appears in this section because the 'listening' child had to attend closely to the information coming over the telephone and ignore everything going on around him. A great many types of material could be used for this activity.*

B   Activities for improving speech

In our discussion in Chapter 1 we showed that a restricted code is likely to be peculiarly inadequate for carrying out certain verbal tasks, such as explanation and the expression of certain types of experience, for example the experience of emotion. We made these tasks and experiences a major focus of the programme. We can

* This type of equipment has been previously used by Martin Deutsch in his compensatory education programmes in the United States, though the activities described above were novel.

list them roughly into five categories: (*a*) extended narrative (*b*) explanation (*c*) detailed and refined description (*d*) the expression of uncertainty and the hypothetical, and (*e*) the description of feelings and relationships between people.

(1) Picture stories

It is not easy to make available in the classroom a large range of experiences for the children to talk about, without considerable extra resources. One technique which was invaluable in exposing the children to new experiences and ideas was that of the picture story. We used this throughout the project, introducing different series and variations in presentation. We wrote the stories ourselves and had them drawn and reproduced for distribution; a frame was made for their presentation.

The picture story consists of four pictures (later we used more) which illustrate a story and are exposed one at a time. The children describe each picture as it appears, and, when all four are exposed, they must retell the sequence as a story. This means that they must include relevant elements and make links between the elements to produce a connected narrative. The teacher uses contributions from all the children initially, finally asking one to produce the complete narrative. The activity works rather better in a small group than it does in a large class. (As we shall see in the next chapter we suggested ways of dividing up the class for group activities, so that the teacher could work with one group.) The difficulty of the tasks was markedly increased during the series, with the children having to contribute more and more themselves.

Series I: Simple action stories

These were the earliest stories used and were very, very simple. Here is one example:

> *Picture One:* Two boys are moving a dilapidated pram from a scrap heap.
> *Picture Two:* The boys are buying a wooden box from a greengrocer.
> *Picture Three:* The boys are hammering the box on to the pram wheels.
> *Picture Four:* The boys are sitting in their new go-kart.

Initially the children can describe each picture to make a simple narrative simply adding 'them' or 'and' or 'when', etc. However, the teacher can show them how it is possíble to build up a more elaborate story by giving names to the characters, appropriate dialogue and more elegant links. For example: Jamie and Peter were on their way home from school when they saw an old pram. It was lying on a scrap heap. 'We could use those pram wheels,' said Peter. 'Let's take it home.' As they took it home, they thought of all the things they could do with the old pram. 'Let's buy a box and make a go-kart,' said Jamie. The next day they counted up their pocket money and went off to the greengrocer's to see if they could find a cheap box. The greengrocer found them an old orange box and sold it to them for sixpence. They took it back to their garden and fetched their father's tools. With a hammer and a few nails they had soon made their go-kart . . . and so on. Children will not produce this degree of elaboration and detail all at once. It takes time. With plenty of examples from the teacher when asked perhaps to produce this story for someone who has not seen the pictures, children can and do make up good stories from simple material.

Series II: Character stories

The next series was also fairly simple and unambiguous. The children were still required to produce a narrative. However, the emphasis in these stories was on the relationships between four characters, their quarrels and coalitions. We produced a whole set of stories, rather like a cartoon series, about the same four characters, two boys and two girls. The children were invited to give names to the characters which they retained throughout the series. For the purpose of illustration here we will call the girls Ann and Carol and the boys Billy and David.

> *Picture One:* Carol, Billy and Ann are playing cricket on an area of waste ground. Their wicket is an old dustbin and their bat a rather inadequate stick. One of them is batting, one is bowling and the other standing behind the wicket. David stands some distance away, watching but not participating.
> *Picture Two:* Carol is seen chasing David away with obvious hostility and the other two are laughing.
> *Picture Three:* The three are still playing cricket but David can be seen approaching the game with a real cricket bat.
> *Picture Four:* The four are playing together with obvious enjoyment. Ann is batting and David is behind the wicket.

It can be seen that the action of the story depends on the motive of the characters. The children decide for themselves why Carol chases David away and the conversation that ensues when David returns with his new cricket bat. It is possible to suggest to the children the mixed reactions of the characters in Picture Three when David returns with his new bat. To relate these elements into a story is a fairly complex task. The subsequent stories show each of the children taking their turn at outsider or as the one having something special.

Series III: Character stories

In the previous series, the action was contingent upon the relations among the characters. The milieu was, however, a familiar one— a group of friends in urban surroundings. In this next series, how- ever, the stories are located in an environment very different from that of the children's, and the characters themselves play widely varying roles. They form a kind of extended family consisting of a grandmother, a younger woman and three children. One of the children is an adolescent, a boy; there is a girl of about ten years and an infant of about eighteen months. A man, probably the father, appears very occasionally in the stories. The stories em- phasize the relationships between the individuals. In every story one character is causing some kind of difficulty which is resolved, if not in this story, then in the subsequent one. Here are two stories from the series:

Story I

Picture One: The scene is the large and beautiful garden of a large and beautiful house. The grandmother is putting leaves and sticks on to a ready-made bonfire. She picks up an old, broken tennis racket and places it on the bonfire too.

Picture Two: The boy and girl come into the garden; one of them is holding a racket and ball, the other is searching around.

Picture Three: They come upon the charred remains of the old racket.

Picture Four: They confront grandmother in great anger.

To construct this story, the children need to decide whether the grandmother's action was deliberate and unkind or whether she made a genuine mistake. The children have already built up a picture of the kind of person grandmother is. In this discussion they should have opinion to bear on this question.

Story II

Picture One: The older boy is tinkering with his bicycle while the baby watches.

Picture Two: The baby has crawled away with the spanner into the house and is banging it against a table leg.

Picture Three: The baby's mother takes the spanner away from the baby, who howls. The grandmother looks through the door.

Picture Four: The grandmother is returning the spanner to the boy with the bicycle.

Here the grandmother is playing a different role from the previous story.

In this and the previous series of picture stories the teacher has ample opportunity to introduce a vocabulary of feeling and motive which may be new to these children. They cannot use simple action-dominated language to describe the events. They must invent dialogue to fit the characters, and furthermore, dialogue to fit the characters' states of mind at any given point in the story.

Series IV: Find the beginning

Restricted code is not amenable to expressing the hypothetical and the tentative. It is a language of assertion. In this series we produced picture stories in which a final picture was exposed first and the antecedent events had to be guessed at. This gave the teacher opportunities for the use of such phrases and words as 'perhaps', 'might', 'if' and so on. As each picture was exposed the interpretations that the children had put forward had to be revised and new ones presented. In fact, the children found it extremely difficult to move backwards in time and reverse the usual procedure. Here is one example of a story presented in reverse order, where the emphasis is less on narrative than on the means of expressing uncertainty:

Picture Four: A boy is taking several lollipops from a jar (or he may be putting lollipops into the jar). The action and his expression are ambiguous, i.e. possibly frightened and he is looking over his shoulder.

Picture Three: The boy's mother (her back facing us) is talking to the boy and pointing towards the door in a direction away from a group of children who are wearing party hats and some of whom are eating lollipops.

Picture Two: Some children in party hats are holding lollipops. Two children, who are without lollipops and are looking rather disagreeable, are holding out their hands towards the boy. To one side is a table with a birthday cake on it and also an empty jar.

Picture One: A group of children wearing party hats are being given lollipops by the boy's mother, who is smiling.

When children first see picture four they usually assume that the boy is stealing the lollipops. In picture three, he may be being excluded from the party for some reason. In picture two there are clearly not enough lollipops to go around. From picture one we can see that the boy's mother is handing out lollipops and will send him to replenish the jar.

In order to increase the reality of different stories possibly having the same endings we designed a series where this was the case. Three different picture stories all had the last picture (picture four) identical. The children were shown the last picture first, had to imagine the antecedent events, and were in turn shown the three alternative versions, guessing at each point what had gone before. Here is an example:

> *Picture Four:* A boy dressed in a track suit is jumping in mid-air; his arms are spread above his head, his face is expressionless. There is no background, i.e. it is white, so that he appears spread-eagled.

> *Picture Three (a):* He is turning a somersault in mid-air against a white background.

> *Picture Three (b):* From below firemen are holding out a big blanket. The boy can be seen above outside the building on the window-ledge preparing to jump.

> *Picture Three (c):* The picture is the same as in picture four but with a slight change in perspective in order to include skis and ski sticks awry on the ground.

> *Picture Two (a):* The boy is upright standing on a trampoline looking pleased. People are standing around watching him and clapping.

> *Picture Two (b):* From inside a room the boy is climbing out through the window. The room is dark and filled with smoke.

> *Picture Two (c):* The boy is skiing down a mountain slope. The scene includes fir trees and chalets.

> *Picture One (a):* The boy is in a gymnasium tying his shoe laces. To one side of this picture is a trampoline against a blank wall. On the other side are ropes, wall bars and other people.

> *Picture One (b):* The boy stands at the top of a staircase; smoke and flames are halfway up, and he looks frightened.

> *Picture One (c):* A mountain scene; a boy sits among a group of people putting on his skis.

Series V: Extended time relations

We returned in this series to an emphasis on finding appropriate devices for an extended narrative, in this case, to indicate time passing. The pictures illustrated a story which was carried on over a long period. This also meant that the children were given an opportunity to invent intervening events themselves, as well as to form them into a coherent story. Here is an example:

Picture One: A mother and father, a boy of about ten and two girls, one of about seven and one about four, are seated around a Christmas tree opening parcels. The boy is holding up an underwater swimming kit of mask and flippers, which he has taken out of a box.

Picture Two: In the boy's bedroom the underwater kit hangs upon the wall. He can be seen playing with other boys. Through the window snow can be seen falling.

Picture Three: An English beach scene by a break-water. The family are sitting on the sand. The boy, wearing his mask and flippers, is wading into the sea. The taller girl in a striped bathing-suit stands holding the hand of the smaller girl. They are watching their brother.

Picture Four: A different beach scene, clearly Mediterranean with pine trees and rocks and striped sunshades. The boy and taller girl, both with underwater swimming gear, are wading into the sea while the smaller girl in the striped costume (the same as in picture three) stands watching them.

Here the children can suggest how the children in the story pass the months before Christmas and the following summer, the interests of the girl in the underwater gear and the promises for a later summer. The pictures are exposed singly. When the children have discussed the story and have added various elements and dialogue, they have to amalgamate it all into a narrative.

Series VI: Reduced cues

In this series the pictures depicted much less action, with the final picture only symbolic or suggestive of a possible ending. By this stage we hoped to have the children inventing stories of their own on the basis of a few hints. In this series all the pictures were exposed simultaneously, and the children were asked to produce a little story from the four pictures immediately. Here is an example:

Picture One: Four children about twelve years old stand around a large snowman who is decorated with a top hat, stick and pipe. The sky is filled with dark clouds.

Picture Two: The children among others are skating on a pond which is fringed with trees and bushes. At the far end, the snowman can be seen. The sky is even darker than in the first picture.

Picture Three: In this picture there is shown only a very round, bright sun (in colour).

Picture Four: A large puddle with a hat and stick floating in it— the sun reflected in the water.

The children can suggest what happened to the children in the pictures, for example, that it was a weekend and they have gone back to school, or that it is the end of winter several weeks later. In these stories there is less possibility of a right answer, and the children are free to invent a great deal.

For every series of picture stories the teachers were supplied not only with the picture and suggested stories but also with suggestions for discussion with the children. These suggestions included details on the pictures that might be overlooked and factual topics introduced into the story. For example, in one story about a baby misbehaving itself, we suggested a discussion about whether babies are 'naughty'. We also included probes for dialogue or elements which needed to be invented.

(2) I-Spy and the surprise boxes

The I-Spy part of this activity was, of course, no novelty of ours. We utilized a well-known game in order to develop two related functions. One of these was to sharpen the discrimination of the children's perception of qualitative and quantitative differences between objects along dimensions of colour, of texture, of shape, etc. The second one was to provide the vocabulary for the expression of these differences. As with the picture stories, the earliest applications of the game were very simple and its difficulty was only gradually increased.

Stage I

The children sit in a semi-circle around the teacher's desk, on which she has placed a number of objects. Initially the clue can be of one attribute belonging to only one object, for example, one purple block. Thus she says 'I spy something which is purple', asking the children to raise their hands when she touches the purple object.

Stage II

She chooses objects which are similar on one dimension but different on others. For example, she might select a number of silver-coloured objects differing in shape and texture. She then says 'I spy something which is silver, slim, flat and rough' (intending a nail file). During the children's guessing she has an opportunity to isolate many attributes while eliminating different objects. For example, one child suggests a sixpenny piece. She points out that the sixpenny piece is flat but round. Another child suggests a milk bottle top. She points out that this is flat but smooth and round.

Stage III

The tasks can be made more difficult by increasing the range of objects, for example, to everything in the classroom. Secondly, the children themselves should be given opportunities for being the I-Spy person.

Stage IV: The surprise boxes

(1) The children work in small groups (the organization of these groups is discussed in the next chapter). One member of each group is handed a closed box with small objects inside it. This child then has to describe the attributes of the object without revealing its identity, which the others must guess.

(2) We also used samples of material a great deal in the programme and for this version of the I-Spy game. The children in the group are each given samples of material, one of which matches the sample in the box. The child being the I-Spy person describes the sample of material according to such qualities as colour, pattern, design and texture, in order that the others may identify the matching piece. (It will be recalled that in the last section a similar game was played using the telephones.) The children do not have to be confined to visual qualities of the objects but can use such tactile attributes as softness, coldness, roughness, etc. A variant of the game using tactile perception can be played as follows: one child is handed a large box with a hole in the lid. The teacher, in view of this child and of the others, puts in a number of objects differing along such dimensions as shape, size and texture. The child puts his hand through the hole, feels *one* object and describes what he can feel to the others who must guess what it is, the teacher correcting wild guesses.

(3) Drama

Drama in the infant school classroom can be considered under at least two categories having different functions. In one category

drama normally involves giving the children the time and opportunity and possibly props to act out in groups their fantasies of
the moment. It is frequently little more than an extension of their
own play, barely modified for performance in front of an audience.
The teacher's role here is minimal.

The second category includes any kind of structured drama, and
can be used for the purposes of language development. We devised
two varieties of structured drama, with one of which most teachers
are probably already familiar. In this latter variety the children
act parts from a story or a poem (in our project these were stories
we had provided for use with the tape-recorder). These parts are
usually elements which have not been included in the story, either
occurring after the story has finished or simply sections of the
story which had no dialogue. The teacher retells the story and
asks the children as a group for their suggestions about what might
be said or done. She then selects a few children to construct a very
short scene, giving them an opportunity to rehearse it. It is then
performed in front of the others. Those watching are invited at the
finish to come and take one of the roles and possibly play it
differently. They are also invited to be fairly critical of what is
said and of how the roles are played, for example, 'the Grandmother was not cross enough' or 'the teacher spoke badly'.

In carrying out this activity the children must select speech which
is appropriate to the role they are playing and the situation which
is being enacted. Thus, it is particularly valuable if the same child
can change roles within the same scene. Furthermore, language
here is obviously a source of control, since the situation proceeds
and is dominated by what the other characters decide to say.

We devised a second variety of structured drama. Here, the
children had to invent the story and the dialogue but were given the
basic situation; in this case a situation where there is a problem
of social relation which has to be solved in the play. Here are
some examples of problems the children were given to act:

(a) Children are skipping in a road and an old lady takes the
     rope and joins in.
(b) Some children find an old typewriter in working condition
     on a rubbish dump. They take it away with them but a
     policeman stops them, thinking they have stolen it.
(c) Some children are buying sweets in a shop. The lady behind
     the counter weighs them, puts them in a paper bag, then
     helps herself to several.
(d) Children on their way home from school see a policeman
     seated on the kerb crying.

It can be seen from these few examples that characters are be-having in a somewhat inappropriate way.* This is part of a deliberate attempt to prevent the children using the ready-made clichés and phrases which they already associate with particular roles and which are, in any case, a formidable part of a restricted code. We wanted to jolt them into finding the language to cope with very unusual situations. We might mention at this point, for the benefit of the sceptical, that the children enjoyed the problems enormously and coped with great originality and inventiveness. The children are simply told the situation. The group are selected to go and resolve the problem and rehearse the scene at the same time. They present their little scene to the others. Again children are invited to come and take over one role, and the scene is played again. The teacher invites criticism of the performance as well as alternative solutions to the problem.

(4) Explanations

In the last chapter we suggested how a teacher might utilize events during the school day, so that children could be asked to give short explanations to the class and to outsiders of what had been happen-ing. In our programme we also used News Time for children to present accounts of how they carried out tasks at home, for example, bathing the dog, making tea, planting flowers or potatoes. In addi-tion, however, we utilized the following techniques for asking children to *instruct* each other verbally.

(5) I-Am-The-Teacher

The children work in pairs, facing each other across two desks which have been put together. A screen is placed between them so that they can talk to each other but neither can see what the other is doing. Each child is given an identical set of materials which can be assembled. One child assembles his materials first. When he has completed his task, he has *verbally* to instruct his partner to produce an identical assembly. He is not allowed to show him. The other child can ask questions but must not look at his partner's assembly. When it is finished the two must compare to see whether the *instructions* have produced similar arrays.

Materials for I-Am-The-Teacher

(a) Dolls furniture, doll figures of adults and children.

* We are indebted to Douglas Young for this notion of role incongruity which we used in several of the programme activities.

(b) Miniature gardens with trees, flowers, benches, etc.
(c) Toy farm.
(d) Wooden shapes (circles, squares, crescents, rods, etc.) of different colours and sizes which adhere by magnetism to a metal board. A picture constructed with these shapes, for example, some sort of animal, cannot be easily determined until all the shapes are in position.
(e) Mosaic pictures.
(f) Spielkarten—these are packs of cards with slots in them so that they can be built into towers. They are like ordinary playing cards but are adapted for building and have on them rather extraordinary designs. They show close-up photographs of needles and pins, miniature dolls, enlargements of insects and familiar objects in strange contexts; all of which give considerable scope for description and discussion.

(6) Using the tape-recorder

In an earlier section we mentioned the use of the tape-recorder to train children to listen to stories. Over time these stories were increased in difficulty and in length. Initially the stories heard on the tape-recorder were repeats of a story previously read by the teacher at the beginning of the week. Later, a group of children who had heard the story together retold it to the class as a group, and the class would corroborate it and correct it where necessary. Children were also asked to listen for particular items of information. In particular the teacher would from time to time read a story without finishing it, and the children would have to listen to the tape to learn the ending and to retell it. Or the teacher would give the children questions which could be answered only by listening to the tape. Finally we produced serialized stories. These, of course, demanded much more from the children in terms of remembering a particular episode and in telling particular parts of the story.

These stories were not selected on the basis of any rigid criteria. They were chosen on the basis of their supposed appeal to a particular age group and were edited to increase the difficulty of the actual language involved. Where there was an emphasis on selection, however, we chose stories in which children behaved in a way out of keeping with their customary roles and where there was a stress on feelings and interpersonal relations.

Throughout the project we had intended to teach the children how to operate the tape-recorder themselves in order to produce their own stories for others to listen to. It was not until the final year, when the children were around eight years old, that this plan was really practicable. Nevertheless, the rehearsing and telling of the story by a group for recording was one of the most creative language activities. Later in school the children have to write stories. At this stage they are already illustrating them. Surely the assumption that later they can carry out the quite difficult task of writing a story rests on the assumption that they are in fact able to tell them, and that they have already had months or even years of producing coherent spoken narrative. If the children can use the tape-recorder, they can listen to their performance critically and change it. They must discuss as a group who will tell which episode, where it is to be dramatized, who will take which part, and so on. They can begin to appreciate that, to be entertaining, the recorded story must run smoothly and coherently. Initially the children retold stories which they had heard already, but some children made up their own stories for presentation in this way. One group of children recorded a story which was told as if through an interview. This activity demands, apart from a tape-recorder, time to be set aside when the group can rehearse and record without interruption or extraneous noise.

(7) Small group discussions

In the last chapter we indicated some classroom activities which could generate discussions. We considered a small group discussion an important opportunity for the teacher to correct faulty constructions and ambiguous phrasing. It is her opportunity for asking a child exactly what he means and helping him to specify it. In fact, in our programme we set aside time for this type of group discussion, suggesting subject matter and activities that the teacher could use. We were interested in getting children to verbalize about hypothetical problem situations ('what would happen if . . .') and to discuss observations which arose in small classroom experiments. The activity required the division of the class into small groups, with the teacher working with one group on discussion. Here are some examples of problem situations which the teacher introduces as 'what would happen if . . .'

Example:
- (a) One morning we got up, and all the clocks everywhere had stopped.
- (b) An old lady knocks at the door of a house which we know is empty. The old lady is deaf and does not hear what we say.

(c) The milkman knocks at the door and asks us to pay for the milk, but we paid a different milkman yesterday.

In all these examples it is possible to produce rather bald one-phrase solutions such as 'go and buy a new clock', but it can lead on to a discussion about primitive ways of keeping time, of life in primitive societies where time has a different significance, and how a clock mechanism works. The 'milkman' example can lead on to a discussion about receipts, about the office work at the dairy, where the money goes and so on. The teacher can also be on the look-out for problems of this sort, preferably genuine ones. She should not operate any premature biases about which problems children may find interesting.

We suggested a number of experiments that the teacher could carry out with small groups. Of course, most teachers already have a programme of such activities; we wanted to stress the opportunity that it provides for learning new words and concepts. We suggested some experiments and the words which children could practise using.

Example 1: Solubility, solution, dissolve, melt. Collect together a number of substances, for example, sugar, salt, aspirin, soap, butter, mud, wood. Which of these will dissolve in water? Give the children an opportunity to say, 'this is soluble; this dissolves; here is the solution of X; we did an experiment investigating solubility, etc.'

Example 2: Air, wind, pressure, buoyancy, vibration, etc. Using a bicycle or balloon pump inflate a paper bag, make soap bubbles. Blow feathers, paper, a recorder, a piece of grass, a dandelion to observe and compare the various effects.

The main point of this activity is to get the children to appreciate the value of words which summarize fairly complex ideas, facts or principles. It is important that the children should actually say the words, in sentences, correctly.

C Activities for improving structure and vocabulary

We turn now to that group of activities where the emphasis is on an intensive training in vocabulary and sentence construction and on the comprehension of logical operations.

(1) Vocabulary
i That reminds me of . . .

Here we used the psychological technique of word association. The teacher starts the game with a word and the children have to say, in turn, 'that reminds me of . . .', giving a word that comes into their minds. If the same word occurs twice, the teacher should suggest a new, unusual word that the similar word reminds her of. The game should be run through rather quickly, the teacher should record new and unusual words, using them as starting-points for later sessions of the game. She should also keep a record of the first and last words that occurred on a particular occasion.

Stage II   That reminds me of . . . because . . . Here each child must verbalize the connection between the word he is given and the word he thinks of. If he cannot do this, then another child can be asked to give a possible link. The primary aim here is to make children aware of words as words and of their conno-tations and conceptual links with other words. We also found that by using masks for this activity we prevented the children looking round the classroom for objects to name rather than think of them.

ii   Alternative statements

The teacher makes a statement to the class, e.g. 'the dog is running down the road'. She then asks the class if they can think of another way of making a similar statement. They probably won't under-stand what she means, and she gives them some examples:

> The dog is running down the road.
> The Alsatian is rushing down the street.
> The hound is racing along the high road, etc.

When a child manages to produce an alternative statement, the others can decide whether the meaning is essentially the same or not. The game thus consists of producing on the one hand as many alternative words in the statement as possible, until someone objects that the statement now means something else. For example, some-one may say, 'the animal is racing along the path'—the teacher can ask whether 'animal' means the same as 'dog' and whether 'path' means the same as 'road'. This activity sensitizes the children to the flexibility of language and to the problem of retaining mean-ing while using different expressions. It also illustrates the way in which words can be classified into superordinate and subordinate categories; apple as an example of fruit, dog as an example of animal, etc. This emphasis on classification was also made in another activity to be described below.

iii Group names and classifications

The teacher names four or five examples of a class or category of object, or a number of objects linked by some common attribute. For example, she can say 'I am going to say five things. You must tell me what is the same about them; sink, bath, bucket, bowl, tank'. The children can reply in terms of a common attribute. In this case they are all used for holding liquid. Or they can reply by classifying the five objects as 'vessels' or 'containers'. The teacher should, of course, start with very easy examples, such as fruit, flowers, animals, means of transport, etc. Later she can graduate to more abstract concepts, for example: 'sad, unhappy, merry, jealous, excited' which can be classified as 'feeling'. Or 'hurrying, rushing, galloping, spinning, whirling' which can be classified as 'rapid movement'.

Stage II The teacher can list five items, one of which does not 'belong' to the others, for example: 'cup, knife, tea-pot, bowl, moon'. She asks the children which item does not 'belong' or is different from the others and why it is different. When the teacher encounters words which are difficult for the children she should explain the concept and, soon after, give another list of items exemplifying that concept. Alternatively she can ask the children to give further examples themselves.

(2) Sentence construction and syntax

i Completion

The teacher provides an incomplete sentence, e.g. 'the jar of marmalade . . .' and asks the children to complete it, each giving a different ending, for example 'the jar of marmalade is full', 'the jar of marmalade is lying on its side', 'the jar of marmalade has a golliwog on the front'. Once the children have grasped the notion of the infinite number of different completions that are possible from a single beginning, the teacher can suggest further elaborations. Thus the teacher gives the single sentence, 'the jar of marmalade was lying on its side'. She then shows by example how such sentences can be added to. She can say, for example, 'When the mother came into the room the jar of marmalade was lying on its side'. The children then make these extensions, each child having to produce different ones. The teacher can place some constraint on the children's contribution by giving them a further word, for example, 'the jar of marmalade was lying on its side/when/but/and/because/yet/under, etc.'

ii Extension

In this game a 'House that Jack Built' structure is required, so that memorization will be an important factor. The class can be divided into two groups. One group can be given a short statement to be extended, for example, 'this is the soldiers' flag'. The other group extends the statement thus, 'this is the soldiers' flag that was blowing in the wind'. The first group continues, 'this is the soldiers' flag that was blowing in the wind that came from the North'. Children from each group in turn volunteer extensions. The teacher can allow controlled prompting from other members of the class in order to keep every child interested and working. The group which is the first to fail to provide an extension or to remember the complete sequence loses. Again this activity must appear competitive to the children, although, in fact, the teacher's aim is to keep as many children involved in the activity as possible.

iii Tenses

The teacher pins on to the blackboard a large picture (she can also draw on the blackboard) illustrating a sentence. For example, the picture might show a boy with his mother and father walking towards the circus tents. The sentence can be something like 'Michael is going to the circus'. She then specifies a time or condition which demands an appropriate use of the verb. Here are some examples:

Next Saturday Michael *is going* to the circus.
Last week Michael *went* to the circus.
If Michael is good he *will/might* go to the circus.
If Michael *had been* good, he *would have gone* to the circus.
When Michael was little he *used to go* to the circus.
If Michael *had* some money he *could go* to the circus, etc.

The wrong use of tense can also be illustrated by the teacher giving some obviously nonsensical statements, for example,
'Next Saturday Michael used to go to the circus', etc.
The teacher should ask individual children to fill in the sentences and not rely on volunteers. The activity should be carried out fairly rapidly for a short period.

iv Construction

The children work in groups. Each group is given a set of picture cards and also a set of word cards. These words are key words for

E

particular constructions, for example: 'if, maybe, whenever, perhaps, sometimes, in case, unless'. The teacher gives each group a key word to use and writes the word on the blackboard. The group then have to use their pictures to make up a sentence using the key word. For example, one group has some pictures indicating (*a*) rain cloud (*b*) children in wellington boots, hats, macks, etc. (*c*) umbrellas. The key word for this group is *whenever*. The children must get together to produce a sentence using the key word and pictures. For example, 'whenever it is raining, the children wear rain-coats, wellington boots and carry umbrellas', The children have a different key word each time, they also exchange pictures fairly frequently too. In our project we produced special cards, both picture and word cards, for this game. However, the teacher can collect picture material – it does not need to be specially constructed. The reader will probably have noticed that in this activity we have introduced written language. A general discussion of where and how the programme involved written work will be found in the next chapter.

(3)   The language of logical operations

The purpose of the following activity, which was designed by Bereiter and Engelmann[15] for work with disadvantaged children in pre-schools in the United States, was to sharpen the children's awareness of the precise meaning of certain linguistic and logical concepts, for example 'and, only, all, not, and not, if, etc.' Initially we used a procedure involving figures drawn on the blackboard. One of the sets of figures was like this:

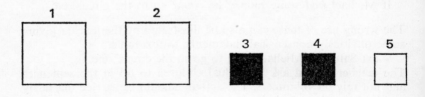

that is, there are two classes of figures, large white squares and small black squares, and an odd one that is small and white.

The teacher proceeds with the following sequence:

(*a*) She describes each item herself.
   'This square is large *and* white.'
   She asks the children to describe each square in these terms;
   pointing to each square, she asks 'What is this square like?'

(*b*) The teacher asks individual children to come to the black-
   board and point to:
   A square that is white.
   A square that is large *and* white.
   A square that is not large *and not* white.
   A square that is large *or* a square that is black, etc.

(*c*) The teacher says 'I am thinking of a square that is not black
   and is not small. Which one am I thinking about?'
   The answer that she wants is, 'You are thinking about
   square one or square two. We don't know which'.
   The teacher says 'I am thinking of a square that is not black
   and not large. Which one am I thinking of?'
   The answer that the teacher wants here is 'You must be
   thinking of square five.'

The children do, of course, see this as a guessing game even where
only one answer is possible, so that each time the teacher should
ask which item she was actually thinking of.

   The teacher says 'I am thinking about all the white squares,
   so which ones (which numbers) am I thinking of?'
   The teacher says 'I am thinking about only one black square.
   Which one am I thinking about?'
   The answer the teacher wants here is 'You are thinking
   about *either* square three or square four'.

(*d*) The teacher points to squares one and two and says 'What
   can I say about these two squares that I can't say about any
   of the others?'
   The answer is 'They are large'. Some children will say 'They
   are large and white'. She must then point out that the little
   square five is also white. She then asks 'If squares are large,
   what else are they?'
   The answer aimed at is 'If squares are large, then they are
   also white'.
   'If a square is black, what else is it?' The answer must be
   'If a square is black, then it is also small'.
   'If a square is white, what else is it?' The answer must be
   'If a square is white, it may also be large or small'.

'If a square is *not* black, what is it?' The answer here must be 'If a square is not black, it is white and it may be large or it may be small'.

It is very important here that the answers are actually said aloud in complete sentences by the children. Initially the children will be repeating a formula. The point is that they are practising saying aloud a logical construction whose truth is illustrated by the figure on the board.

The teacher can and should change the form of the model without changing its basic content. For example the following figures serve equally well:

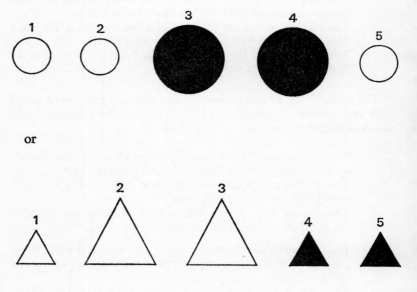

or

and the two colours can be drawn from a large number of combinations for which she has coloured chalk available.

This particular game should not be carried out for very long in any one session. We suggest less than ten minutes but more than five, since it requires sustained attention and activity on the part of the children. When the children have become familiar with the requirements of the task, the teacher can introduce the following game.

The Game All that is needed is a miniature set of ordinary playing-cards. Each child in the class has any six playing-cards. The teacher will ask the children to hold up cards on the following instructions:

(1) Hold up a red card.
(2) Hold up a card that has a black and a three.
(3) Hold up any card with a three *or* a four *or* a five.
(4) Hold up a card that is *not* a diamond.
(5) Hold up a card that is *not* a diamond *and not* a spade.
(6) Hold up all red cards.
(7) *If* you have a red card, *then* hold it up.
(8) *If* you have *only/all* red cards, hold them up.
(9) If you have a red card *and* it is *not* a diamond, hold it up.
(10) *If* you do *not* have a black card, hold up a red.

The instructions illustrated for the card game and for the proceeding game do not exhaust all the logical possibilities or all the possibilities provided by the materials. The teacher will think of more. It is useful, however, to have prepared a set of instructions previous to any one session. When the children are familiar with the game, two or three can come to the front of a class to monitor the performance of the others and to spot mistakes. Later still children can give the instructions themselves.

In summary, the activities that have been described here were designed to improve and extend the language of children who are probably confined to a restricted code. The activity covered three types of language function where restricted code is particularly inadequate. Firstly we aimed to improve their attention to speech and to be more aware and critical of what they hear others say. Secondly we set up language tasks with which such children would be rather unfamiliar. Thus we emphasized tasks which required (*a*) sustained connected narratives, (*b*) the expression of uncertainty and the hypothetical, (*c*) refined and detailed descriptions, (*d*) the verbalization of feelings, motives and interpersonal relations, and (*e*) explanations taking into account an uninitiated and unfamiliar listener. Thirdly we introduced activities to rapidly extend the children's repertoire of lexis and structure.

(4) Basis skills

One final point must be made. The period of the project was one during which children were acquiring the basic skills of reading and writing. Our emphasis was always on spoken language as the ultimate basis for written language. Early in the project we made no attempt to relate this work to other work on basic skills. By the end of the second year, however, it seemed relevant to have the children use material from the language programmes, particularly, for example, stories in their written work. In fact, we provided some special books for this purpose. We provided work folders and paper and a very large range of picture postcards, mostly of paintings, to be distributed to each child. In this folder the children drew pictures illustrating a made-up story which was told to the class. They also made up stories on the basis of picture postcards. Initially these stories were told aloud, then the card was attached to the folder and the story was written with the help of the teacher. In this folder one section was divided off for explanations. Here they noted in writing some common classroom procedures. For example, 'What happens at meal times?', and also descriptions of simple tasks like 'making tea', 'playing snakes and ladders or hide-and-seek', i.e. descriptions which they would have practised orally for some time previously.

The children were also given a book to be used as a dictionary. The basis of classification was not alphabetical but decided in discussion with the teacher. For example, most children used class concepts as a basis for classification, for example 'animal', 'machinery', etc. Others however classified words in terms of grammatical functions, yet others in terms of some external attribute like colour or size. Whichever classification they used they had to make a little index which was, where possible, illustrated. The aim was not simply to collect and spell words but to increase the children's awareness of words in various conceptual and functional hierarchies; to think not only of what a written word denotes or means, but the many attributes of the thing that it means. An 'elephant' can be classified in terms of a concept 'animal'—probably the most common classification—but it can also be classified as 'large', examples of the class among which belong skyscrapers, pine trees and liners; it can also be classified as 'unusual', things we don't meet often like meteors, orchids, magicians and large balloons. The recording of these words in this way is linked with the oral vocabulary game described in the chapter. Of course the teachers were encouraged to emphasize correct spelling and clear writing in this activity as they would in any other. This chapter now provides sufficient information on the language programme activities for us to be able to describe exactly how they were carried out in the classroom, the equipment we provided and all the important practical details. Before turning to these matters in the next chapter, we shall conclude this one with a list summarizing all the activities used in the language programme.

Summary of the language programme

A   Activities for improving attention and auditory discrimination

(1) The O'Grady game

    i.
    ii.
    iii.

(2) Listening in the dark

    i.   *Recognizing voices.*
    ii.   *Silly sentences.*
    iii. *Rhymes and poems.*
    iv. *What did I say?*
    v.   *Remembering in the dark.*
    vi. *The tape-recorder.*

(3) Instruction chains

(4) Telephones

B   Activities for improving speech

(1) Picture stories

    Series I.   *Simple action stories.*
    Series II.   *Character stories.*
    Series III. *Character stories.*
    Series IV. *Find the beginning.*
    Series V.   *Extended time relations.*
    Series VI. *Reduced cues.*

(2) I-Spy and surprise boxes

(3) Drama

(4) Explanations

(5) I-Am-The-Teacher

(6) Using the tape-recorder

(7) Small group discussions

C   Activities for improving structure and vocabulary

(1) Vocabulary

    i.   That reminds me of.
    ii.   Alternative statements.
    iii. Group names and classification.

(2) Sentence construction and syntax

    i.   Completion.
    ii.   Extension.
    iii. Tenses
    iv.   Construction.

(3) The language of logical operations

(4) Basic skills

Chapter 5 Behind the Scenes

We have already stressed that an important feature of the language programme was that any teacher who had been normally trained should be able to run it in her own classroom as a part of her daily teaching schedule. We therefore made *no* attempt to select teachers for participation in the project. Those who took part had been assigned to their particular classes by their headteachers in the usual manner. This resulted in a considerable range in experience and age among the project teachers; we had teachers with more than ten years' experience as well as those who had come straight from colleges of education. With regard to E1 teachers, we did not feel at any time that either of these factors, age and experience, was in any way related to success in administering the language programme. All teachers concerned with the project were qualified. We were very fortunate in that none of the E1 teachers declined to participate in the project, though perhaps naturally enough some evinced considerable apprehension and anxiety in the early weeks.

The seminars

The teachers were invited initially to attend weekly seminars at the local youth centre immediately after school to discuss problems of infant school teaching, with a view to participating in an experimental research programme. For each attendance they were paid a fee equivalent to payment for two hours' teaching. The seminar group was made up of the three reception class teachers, the three teachers who would be taking over from them in the second year and two members of the research team. In the second year of the project the three Junior school teachers who were to take the children in the third and final year joined the group, whilst the reception class teachers continued to attend from time to time. For the final year of the project only the second- and third-year teachers attended. This meant that throughout the project we maintained a seminar group not only large enough to provide diversity of contributions but which guaranteed continuity of involvement in the project. The C2 teachers also attended fortnightly seminars with Professor Bernstein. We shall leave a detailed discussion of these till the next chapter.

During the first term of the project, while the children were settling in and were being assessed for intelligence and linguistic ability, the weekly seminars revolved around the topic of language and its importance for intellectual development. The major focus of discussion was the underachievement of children in working-class areas and the ways in which the problem might be tackled. These early seminars then had a number of functions. Firstly they enabled us to sensitize the teachers to the linguistic problems of lower working-class children, to acquaint them with the facts available in the literature in this area, and to introduce them to the methods and problems of educational research. Secondly they sensitized us to the problems and needs of the teachers who already felt themselves overburdened with classes of forty children, ranging in ability from the very bright to the educationally subnormal and in speech from the insistent to the non-English speaking immigrants. And, most importantly, the seminars enabled us to build up a relationship of confidence and mutual trust which we considered essential for the success of the project. We felt that it would be impossible to run an explanatory language programme of the sort we envisaged, if we tried to impose our ideas on the teachers from without and initiated the programme in the form of demands veiled as requests. We also believed that whilst the teachers had much to learn from us, we in turn had a great deal to learn from them. Consequently, our aim throughout the lifetime of the project was to work with the full support and co-operation of the teachers by encouraging and profiting from their own contributions. In this aim we feel we were largely successful. This does not mean that for three years everything ran smoothly. From time to time, of course, as in any joint venture, there were disagreements, expressions of dissatisfaction, feelings of hostility and of personal inadequacy. But the very fact that the seminars provided a forum for the ventilation of feelings as well as opinions made the idea of co-operation and joint contribution a reality and not simply an empty phrase.

Out of these early seminars evolved the twenty-minute daily language programme, and from the second term onwards they were taken up mainly with the running of the programme. In these work meetings day-to-day problems encountered in the classroom were discussed, criticisms and suggested modifications of current activities were made, and ideas for new activities were put up for consideration.

Visits to the school

Once a week one of the two researchers called in at each of the three schools to see the programme in operation. This at first created some anxiety on the part of the teachers, who perhaps only naturally felt themselves to be as much under observation as the programme. However, these feelings were soon dispelled by the active participation of the visiting researcher in the programme. By taking an active role during these visits in helping the teacher to conduct the language games and activities, we arrived at a much better understanding of what was and was not possible at any stage in the project. Through first-hand experience we came to know the limitations of the children and the practicality of each part of the programme. This was a much better way of learning than would have been available through discussion or even passive observation. We were greatly indebted to the headteachers in allowing us to work in their schools in such an informal manner. This shared experience in running the programme gave in turn substance and meaning to the subsequent seminar discussions, which they would not otherwise have had. The teachers very soon appreciated the importance of this monitoring of the programme by us and welcomed the visits. To give a simple example, we found very early in the project that the position of the teacher during News Time was very important in determining the degree of involvement and participation of the class in this activity. If the teacher sat in front of the class, then the child reporting his news tended to address the teacher exclusively and often in a tone that was scarcely audible to children at the back of the class. If, on the other hand, the teacher sat at the back and stressed the importance of addressing the whole class, then the child reporting from the front of the class had to raise his voice to encompass the whole class in his delivery. This in turn had the effect of stimulating the class to ask questions and comment on the news. In the first case News Time tended to be a dialogue, in the second there was often a discussion. The importance of this simple (and perhaps to the reader obvious) piece of stage management by the teacher was not so obvious to those caught up in the situation of the moment. It came to their notice only through the monitoring visits of the researchers. The subsequent improvement in News Time was striking.

Aids for the teachers

In the preceding chapter we described the language games and activities which we used during the three years of the project. It should be noted that we have included only the successful ones. There were in fact a number of activities which we thought up and tried out, but which the teachers soon rejected as impractical or the children found too difficult or uninteresting. We consider there would be little point in describing those explorations which failed. Nor, however, do we consider that those activities which we did find useful are necessarily the only ones that a teacher could use to enrich the language of her pupils. They were simply the ones that we happened to think up or chose to work with.

The language programme was introduced into the classrooms at the beginning of the Spring term, when the children had had one term of schooling. Each teacher was provided with a work manual containing a description, rationale and instructions for administration of each activity. This manual was revised four times during the three years to meet the changing needs of the children, to incorporate modifications to ongoing activities and to introduce new ones. These manuals constituted the hard core of the programme from which the teachers worked. The preceding chapter of the book is a combined summary of these manuals.

In addition to the manuals the teachers were supplied with handouts for particular activities, from week to week. These were used by them whenever they were at a loss for time, or ideas, or even vocabulary. They were quite optional and served simply as occasional props which we initially introduced at the teachers' own request. For example, each picture story was accompanied by a typescript giving a description and interpretation of the story, vocabulary of content and suggestions for questions and discussion. This became more useful as the picture stories increased in ambiguity and was particularly important in orienting the discussion towards the emotional and motivational states of the characters portrayed. All stories recorded on tape were accompanied by a typed transcript; lists of problem situations for the children to resolve in drama were provided from time to time; and in many of the activities involving sentence construction by the teacher there were lists of possible sentences, should the teacher run out of ideas.

Changes in the classroom

Earlier in this chapter we mentioned that there was no prior selection of teachers for the project, because we wished the programme to be run under normal conditions. For the same reason the project classrooms were neither specially designed nor changed in any significant manner. The only structural alteration consisted of a small baffle-board partition erected in one corner of the classroom which acted as a screen between children listening to the tape-recorder and the rest of the class.

On the other hand, we made important and necessary changes in the social structure of the classes. It will be obvious to the reader from the preceding chapter that some of the programme activities could be conducted with the whole class but others could only take place in small groups, and in some cases between pairs of children. A major problem besetting any teacher with a class of forty children is that she is unable to spend enough time talking to individual children. Even for the most conscientious teacher sensitive to the importance of talking individually to children there is just not time enough in the day to fulfil this need. The problem is often made more serious by the deplorable but totally unconscious manner in which many teachers tend to interact only with the brighter, more verbal children during class teaching periods. Every teacher, of course, faces the problem of deciding at whose pace a lesson is to be conducted. If the slower, duller, less verbal children call the pace, the brighter children get impatient, fidgety and noisy. If, on the other hand, the brighter, more verbal children call the pace, the spiral of underachievement gathers momentum as the noise and fidgeting of the less able children begins to take on a permanent character. Anyone who has taught in a large class will recall how difficult it is to ignore the bright, eager faces, up-stretched hands and insistent voices crying 'Miss!, Miss!', and patiently wait for and guide the less able pupil to produce an answer, an example, an idea or a suggestion.

Within the context of the language programme we tried to reduce the seriousness of the problem by running a series of concurrent group activities. From the beginning of the programme in the Spring term the teachers divided their classes into work groups of five children. These groups were identified with a name and remained fairly stable over the three years. The groups were composed of sample and non-sample children. Initially, of course, each group activity had to be taught to the class as a whole. This was usually done by using one group as a demonstration group with the rest of class observing, and occasionally, with more difficult activities, the teacher had to instruct each group separately over the course of several days. Once group activities were running autonomously, the teacher was freed from all but minimal supervision of the class and was thus able to deal with any particular group having difficulty, to settle disputes, to encourage performance and, most important, to converse with a small number of children at a time, thereby introducing new ideas, new vocabulary and new constructions. In other words, the teacher tended to circulate among the groups during the twenty minutes of the programme, stopping to intervene where she felt it most necessary.

To anyone accustomed to the idea of the classroom as a place of quiet, serious study with only one voice to be heard at a time, the noise level in the project classroom would have seemed unthinkable. The programme was essentially a talking programme, and you cannot have five or six discussion groups in one large room without a considerable amount of noise. However, whilst to someone entering the classroom the noise might be rated as rather a din, to the children and teacher engaged in the activities the noise was no more noticeable than it is to groups of people talking at a cocktail party.

Though the composition of the groups remained fairly stable over the three years, we did carry out one major change early on. Initially the groups had been formed by the teachers of children deemed by them to be of different levels of ability. That is, each group contained a mixture of bright and not so bright children, in the belief that the former would be able to help the latter. However, after a term of the programme we concluded on the basis of our own and the teacher's observations that in each of the three E1 classes there were a few children who were neither participating in nor benefiting from the programme. In several cases it seemed that the children were simply not able to perform as quickly as other members of their groups, and in the case of sample children their lack of ability was reflected in the intelligence test results obtained in the Autumn term. In other cases it seemed to be not so much a matter of intelligence as of personality; particularly shy or withdrawn children were simply swamped by the more dominant and vociferous members of their groups. Accordingly we decided to set up in each of the three classes what soon came to be called among ourselves 'the non-talkers' group, composed of the five or six children who contributed little or nothing in their own groups. We believed that the creation of these special groups would have two advantages. In the first case, the children in them would become more salient for the teachers and thus receive more attention and help from them than children in other groups. Secondly, some of the children in these special groups would be forced to take up more assertive roles than they had been able to take up previously.

Basic skills

A factor which placed considerable constraints on our plans for a language programme was the short duration of the time allotted to it each day. We settled for twenty minutes per day (an hour and forty minutes per week) in consultation with the project teachers during the early seminars. We all felt that, given the exploratory nature of the programme and the fact that the sample children would only have two years in the infant school, we could not legitimately take up too much time, from the well-established activities on the school timetable. The children had to master the basic skills of reading, writing and numeracy in two years and be able to compete with three-year children as soon as they entered the Junior school. In theory, unless a child can read and write when he enters Junior school, he will be unable to follow the curriculum. Teachers in Junior schools do not receive any training in the teaching of reading, though they soon get plenty of experience. It is not unusual in working-class areas for as much as a third of the two-year children entering Junior school to be illiterate. We did not expect that in the first two years of schooling our purely oral language programme would have any positive effect on the children's literacy, though we would expect it later in their school career. On the other hand, it was always possible that we might have a negative effect during this time, simply because we were taking up an hour and forty minutes of class time each week. To satisfy ourselves and the teachers on this point we gave a reading test to all children in the sample during the third and fourth week of their first term in the Junior school. The test used was the Neale Analysis of Reading Ability[16] which provides separate measures for rate, accuracy and comprehension. Whilst the results showed nearly one quarter of the children to have reading ages a year behind their chronological ages and, for the purposes of the Junior school curriculum, to be still non-readers, there was no difference between E1 group and the two Control groups of schools. We concluded that whilst the results were no cause for celebration, they did conform to our expectations and showed that our intervention had not had a negative effect on the children's literacy.

Timing of activities

Since the games and activities which we have described in Chapter 4 covered a period of three years' schooling, they were pitched at different age levels. Some lasted the whole of the three years, but the materials changed continuously and the level of difficulty increased. Some were introduced, found to be too difficult, dropped from the programme and reintroduced later at a more appropriate age. Yet others were introduced, lasted for a short while and were reintroduced from time to time as revision. The chart below shows

	INFANTS		JUNIOR	
	FIRST YEAR	SECOND YEAR	THIRD YEAR	
	Autumn Spring Summer	Autumn Spring Summer	Autumn Spring Summer	
Teachers' seminars	←———————————————————————————→			
Picture stories	←—————————————————————→			
Tape-recorded stories	←————————————————————→			
Telephones	←————————————————————→			
I-spy	←—————————————→			
O'Grady	←———- - - - - -→			
Listening in the dark		←—————————————→		
I'm the teacher		←————————————→		
Drama		←—————————————→		
Instruction chains		←——————- - - - -→		
Sentence construction and syntax		←—————————————→		
Alternative statements		←—————————————→		
Group names and classification		←————————————→		
Explanation			←——————————→	
Logical operations			←————————→	
Group discussion and experiments			←————————→	
Tape-recording			←————————→	

the time span occupied by each of the major kinds of activity. Broken arrows indicate periods when activities were occasionally revised. False starts are not indicated, so that unbroken arrows represent periods when activities were an established part of the programme.

Chapter 6 Evaluation: Theoretical

In Chapter 2 we described how the project was set up as an experiment, to investigate the effects of giving children daily extra language work. Initially, of course, we did not know whether it was possible, practically, to produce such a programme. It had to be carried out by teachers not specially trained and without great expense or extra equipment; it had to be supervised from a small part of the research unit with limited resources. This meant that the project was an exploratory one. An important outcome has been the demonstration that the programme could be carried out under the constraints we have mentioned. By a process of discussion and co-operation with the teachers we produced a programme that could be carried out with a large class. In fact the teachers themselves were so enthusiastic about the programme that they asked for copies of the materials we had made and continued the activities with new children after they had left the project. Some of them even continued to attend seminars with new project teachers. We feel that this demonstration by the teachers, that the project was really operable, is most encouraging. The main reason why the project was set up in the form of an experiment was, of course, that we had to assess the effects on the children of participation in the programme. This assessment was extremely difficult, and we could not carry it out entirely to our satisfaction. Since this book is intended primarily for teachers, we shall spend some time discussing why evaluation was so difficult. We hope that this discussion will not only give the reader an insight into the problems of the present research project but a better understanding of research in education generally, and perhaps enable him to make a critical appraisal of any projects in which he may at some time participate.

Firstly, then, we will discuss problems which are encountered in experimental evaluation and then in a later section describe what we actually did.

In the ideal psychological experiment a number of adult individuals are herded into the laboratory for a small fee. Let us suppose the experimenter is interested in the development of special techniques for training in the decoding of messages. He wants to find out whether these training techniques have any effect on the subjects' subsequent performance on message decoding. First he will divide his subjects into two groups. One group will receive the training, the other will not. The first group will be called the experimental group, the second will be called the control group.

During the experiment these latter subjects will either do nothing at all or they will be given some task like threading needles or matching cardboard shapes. The task, anyway, will be irrelevant to the problem of decoding messages. Both groups of subjects will then be tested on a task of decoding messages. Perhaps the experimental group will show distinct superiority at the task. A reasonable interpretation of this superiority might involve the special training procedures. However, even this simple-sounding experiment involves a number of hidden problems which the reader will perhaps have detected. For example, it is just possible that the experimenter divided his subjects in such a way that one group was composed of individuals who were superior in intelligence, or even superior at message decoding, before the experimenter began the training procedures. If the experimental groups had been superior initially, then he could not confidently attribute their performance to his training procedures. However, he can get round this problem by not only randomly assigning subjects to groups but by testing their ability to ensure that they are comparable. Comparable in what respect? We might suppose that they ought to be comparable in intelligence. On the other hand, even if they were, then one might still have one group containing many subjects unusually good at message decoding. The experimenter, then, will devise some little test of message decoding and ensure that his groups are roughly comparable in this ability. This simple example serves to introduce one of the besetting problems in our more complex project. We had to ensure that the children in the nine schools, that is in the three experimental and six control schools, were comparable at the onset of the project. On what dimensions had our project children to be comparable? Firstly, we wanted them to be similar in intelligence. However, our project was only indirectly concerned with general intelligence; we were concerned primarily with linguistic skills. Therefore, they needed to be comparable with respect to linguistic development. Over and above these considerations, we felt that class and environmental factors should be taken into account. It was necessary to have schools drawn from similar areas with children of similar backgrounds. One reason being, of course, that environmental variables may have overriding influences regardless of language or any other special training.

Now, in our ideal example, these initial assessments are made before the experiment starts. However, it takes weeks to test the intelligence of children in nine schools and to analyse the scores. It takes months or even years to collect, transcribe and analyse the recorded speech of children. Consequently, although the schools and groups were matched and comparable in terms of social class and environmental variables, the time available for our project was limited, so that we started with no more than the pious hope that children would be comparable in the relevant skills. In support of this decision to go ahead there seemed no special reason why the children should be very different in ability; they had, after all, similar backgrounds. However, as we have seen in Chapter 2, they were not similar. The results of the analysis of the intelligence data, available some time after the programme had started, showed E1 group children to be unpredictably higher on verbal tests. In addition, there were large differences between different schools within each experimental group. To take into account these initial differences when assessing subsequent change is statistically rather complex. In the next chapter we will describe how we attempted it.

In our example the experimenter interprets superior performance by his experimental group subjects in terms of their special training. Since they are adults and the duration of the experiment is short, he has no reason to suppose that other changes will be taking place. In our project the subjects were children and the duration of the project rather long. Two types of change had to be interpreted. Changes could occur as a result of experimental treatment; but changes would also be occurring as a function of development. Our subjects' intellectual capacities would be expanding rather rapidly through growth. Now, of course, we arranged to have two control groups. The subjects here could change in performance only as a result of growing older. Our experimental group should show increments over and above this, as a result of language training. However, some caution is needed in making this assumption. We do not know that intellectual development proceeds in a smooth, even fashion. For example, children shown to be less 'bright' on tests at one stage may be developing temporarily at a different rate to children of apparently higher ability at that stage. This point illustrates again the importance of matching subjects initially. Children performing at an optimal level cannot show as much improvement through training as children performing suboptimally. Then it has to be stressed that, if a language training programme produces changes in children, there are many ways in which these changes will show. We may improve the abilities of children at present performing sub-optimally. We may arrest the later deterioration of children performing optimally at present. The point is that changes over time in an experiment of this sort are extremely difficult to interpret.

We have mentioned throughout this book two groups of schools comprising two control groups. In our example it will be remembered that the experimenter could use his control group in at least two ways. He wants to make sure that they do not participate in the experimental programme. If he leaves them alone it is just possible that they will alleviate their boredom by practising impromptu mental games of message decoding, particularly if they have some suspicion about the nature of the experiment. Or they may have a little rest, in which case the experimental group may be penalized on the test by the fatigue of having participated in the experimental training. There are a number of possibilities. The experimenter decides that it is safer to give them something to do. This will fatigue them, possibly alleviate their boredom, and probably prevent them mentally practising message decoding tasks. An important point is that the experimenter has a good idea of what his control group are hearing, doing, and seeing, that is, he has 'controlled' as far as possible for extra factors which would vitiate his experiment.

In our project we had to assume that the only difference between our experimental and control schools was the operation of a language training programme in the former. Of course, this assumption could not be justified. It is extremely difficult to obtain a 'pure' control group in educational research.

We set up two types of control schools. In the C2 schools we attempted to control the so-called Hawthorne effect. It has been observed by researchers in industry as well as education that the simple knowledge of being selected for a project is sufficient to change a subject's performance. He will do more work because he suddenly and inexplicably feels 'keener'. This is particularly true in education. A teacher who thinks she is being observed or offered a chance to try out new work will often step up her performance. In psychology we call this process 'an increase in motivation'.

In our C2 schools the teachers were invited to participate in seminars to discuss many aspects of infant school teaching. These seminars were conducted by Professor Bernstein. The teachers were paid for attendance and were given an opportunity to carry out small projects and investigations in the classroom, which then became the topics for discussion in the seminars. Topics relating to language were not introduced and did not spontaneously arise. We thought that these measures would make C2 teachers and children comparable to E1 teachers and children with respect to motivation. The C1 schools were left alone, apart from the various testing procedures. The reader will, of course, argue that C1 teachers knew that they must be in a project. This is perfectly true. However, we argued hopefully that we might see some invariant order of performance, with E1 always the best, followed by C2 and then C1. If C1 thought they were in a project, it was certainly a less exciting project than C2 thought that they were in. We thus made an attempt to control for increased motivation in E1 schools. However, changes in motivation are among many that can take place in a school over a three year period. Unlike the experimenter in our example, we cannot lock up our children and teachers for three years and isolate them from outside influences. Our school may experience sudden and temporary staffing problems. One school may be in the middle of a rebuilding project and the children housed in a small and unsuitable classroom. A group of children may experience change from a 'laissez-faire' to a rather strict teacher, or vice-versa. Any of these events may depress or accelerate the children's performance in an uncontrollable way. In our project both the headmistress and class teacher in one control school were unusually interested in language development without knowing anything about our project at all. In yet another control school a teacher arrived from abroad with a brisk programme aimed at language development for the lower working-class child. Of course, we could not stop excellent teaching going on in control schools. It was not within the terms of the project. In fact, children in both these schools showed a higher than expected performance later on. Our attempts to create control groups were not very successful, and one doubts whether this can be fully achieved in any research carried out within normally functioning schools, except in very large projects using many schools.

A problem rather similar to the one just discussed is that of variation in experimental treatments. In our imaginary experiment the experimenter alone carries out the training procedures. He can be reasonably certain that his presentation is the same for all his subjects, even though some of them may suffer occasional lapses of attention and miss something that has been said. Over the three years of the project nine different teachers were involved in the operation of our programme. The teachers changed with each school year. The final year involved a change of head as well when the children moved into the junior school. It would be quite absurd to imagine that these teachers handled the programme very similarly.

Each had her particular style and preferences for some activities rather than others. Again it was not within the terms of the project for us to try and impose an inflexible teaching method. We could not carry out the programme without their help and co-operation; we relied on them to show us what was practicable and which activities were not really enjoyed by the children. If one teacher, in spite of general consensus, found particular activities disagreeable or difficult, she was likely either to underemphasize them or not to do them well. Thus, there was a distinct limit to our control over the presentation of the programme. There was also a limit to our control over the children's reception of it. For one thing, children are absent from school at various times. Some of them are absent a great deal. Even were this not the case, individual children's participation in any activity fluctuates a great deal through a number of factors. The main point is obvious, namely, that both presentation of the programme by the teacher and reception of it by the children varied quite uncontrollably and in a way that does not occur in the more rigorous laboratory experiment.

We have mentioned that to measure change due to a special training procedure we test our subjects initially to ensure that they are of comparable ability; after the training procedure we test them again to see whether the groups now differ in performance. We may compare their performance on the first test with that on the second. There are a number of possible procedures. However, this description glosses over a rather difficult problem. Supposing in our imaginary experiment we haven't the time to teach our subjects every possible coding arrangement. We select a few for training, believing that these training examples will inculcate the principle sufficiently for our subjects to tackle other decoding tasks. If we simply tested them using the identical items used in the training, we would not be very excited at the experimental group's superior performance. We would want to have improved some more general skill. The problem is to decide how far-ranging the test items can be from the original training. Perhaps another example will illustrate the problem more clearly. Supposing it is possible to train children to obtain higher quotients on intelligence tests. Unless these higher quotients are accompanied by other changes as well, we would not consider them very valuable. How though do we specify what these changes would be and develop tests to measure them? Chapter 4 has shown our programme to cover a rather wide range of activities. The changes wrought in the children might range from a larger vocabulary or more frequent correct use of the past tense to improved social adjustments and some highly original poetry. How should we measure change in the children's ability? We will take up the problem again when we describe what was actually done.

There is another related problem. On the basis of the initial tests we have tried to assign our subjects to groups which are comparable in ability. These initial tests must be relevant to the skills we are hoping to improve. But they can't be identical, since the subjects aren't supposed to have them yet. When we test the subjects afterwards we obviously want to test them on something more extensive. Not only that, if people do a test once, when they repeat they are usually better at it anyway, even without special training. They learn something just from doing the test. Now one can argue that both groups will be better on the 'after test' but the experimental group will be much better. With child subjects the problem is rather more difficult than this—because, as we mentioned earlier, their intellectual capacities will improve anyway, but not at a very predictable rate. The increment or lack of it on the post-test by the experimental group is difficult to interpret. On the whole we would prefer to use different pre- and post-tests.

In our imaginary example the subjects are tested at the end of the training session, and the experimental group show a definite superiority. However, supposing the experimenter happened to get all his subjects together again six weeks later for testing. He might find that the superiority of the experimental group had been very short-lived. Perhaps their superior skills had only lasted a few days. The importance of this would, of course, depend on the purposes for which training was being developed. In the case of our own project the problem is more serious. We might, for example, show large effects after six months of special training and ever smaller effects during the succeeding year. Perhaps the effects might not even outlive the project. Ideally, with unlimited research funds, children would be frequently tested and the survival of effects assessed through follow-up studies into secondary school. This was impossible, and the only testing carried out was during the project. The timing of these tests was not dictated by theoretical considerations at all. In fact other members of the research unit were invading the schools for various purposes, and we tested when such an invasion would not be too disturbing or follow too closely on a previous one.

Our project differed from the laboratory experiment in that over the three years a fair number of our subjects began to disappear. Children moved to different schools in the same area or moved out of the area altogether. We were worried at one point that this loss of the sample might be selective, i.e. 'brighter' children might be moving away to better areas. However, this was not the case. As has been shown in an earlier chapter the initial test scores for children who later moved out did not differ from that of the sample at large. However, it did present a problem in the sense that it became increasingly difficult to find appropriately matched children for testing. For example, owing to the initial variability, we had to take sub-samples of children from the different groups matched for sex and performance on one of the initial tests. This meant that some children were being repeatedly tested and others not tested at all, because we couldn't match them. At one point there were only two boys in one of our sample control school classes. This kind of sub-sampling is open to serious objections.

We can summarize by saying that our experiment deviated from the ideal in a number of ways. These fall into three categories. In the first category are the elements of uncontrolled variation. These include variability in the subjects' initial ability with school and group biases; variability in teachers' presentation and in the children's reception of the programme, which, together with other external influences, are factors which would affect the children's progress. With so few schools involved, a bias affecting one school could mask any effects occurring from a special programme. In a large-scale project involving many schools these sources of positive and negative bias are more likely to be balanced across the experimental and control groups, so cancelling each other out. Change due purely to experimental treatment is much more easily detectable in the large experiment. In the second category are the purely circumstantial problems of loss of sample children, attenuated testing and so forth. In the third category are the more theoretical problems related to the nature of the changes themselves. What kinds of changes in abilities could we reasonably expect and what kind of tests would best measure these changes? We now take up this problem in a little more detail in the following chapter where we will describe the evaluation experiments.

Chapter 7   Evaluation: Practical

In Chapter 6 we discussed some of the problems involved in carrying out an experiment in an educational context. Such experiments are usually concerned with discovering the effects of different methods of teaching or different types of work arrangement; one is observing changes in the subjects as a result of exposure to some new procedure. We have shown that the evaluation of such changes is not very easy.

One problem is that of specifying exactly what changes should have occurred. If we introduce new methods of learning to read, we evaluate their efficiency in terms of such measures as average reading age in the experimental group as compared with that of the control group. We may expect other changes too—for example, better behaviour in the classroom by early readers. However, the main prediction is clear and we can investigate subsidiary predictions, if we have the time and the money.

In our research project we aimed at improving language skills generally. What do we mean by language skills? At the simplest level we might mean possession of a large vocabulary. Even this definition is not so simple. For example, by 'large vocabulary' we may mean the ability to give definitions of uncommon words, or we may mean the ability to match a definition given pictorially or verbally with the appropriate words. Some tests of verbal intelligence are constructed from measures such as these. However, it is possible that a child might possess a large vocabulary (as defined in these ways) without using it very effectively when he talks or writes. Furthermore, vocabulary is only one aspect of language skill. There are many words which have important logical and operative functions, but which would not be included in tests of vocabulary. The ability to use these words and a variety of syntactic structures appropriately is an index of verbal development.

Although during the last ten years considerable work has been invested in analysing the development of syntax in young children, we do not yet have developmental scales of language. In contrast, there are several tests of general intelligence which have been developed and standardized on large populations of children. This means that with an intelligence quotient we can describe a child's ability with respect to the rest of the population of his age. No similar quotient exists for language development. We can only give a rough and rather subjective description of a child's language skills at any particular age. Why is there an absence of standardized language tests? One reason is that we cannot agree on appropriate scoring procedures. Let us suppose that we record a child's speech in some kind of interview. We can count the total number of words he uses, or better still, the number of different words he uses. We can count the number of complex verb constructions which appear, or perhaps the subordinate clauses. However, the way in which one weights the appearance of particular items in a child's speech depends on one's theory of grammar, and ultimately upon the knowledge of the developmental stage at which these normally occur. To give a simple example, supposing one child presents many varied adjectives and adverbs but few complex verb constructions. How shall we compare his performance with that of the child who uses many complex constructions but who is sparse on the adjectives and adverbs? The fact is that we cannot yet assign a single score for language development in the way that we can for general intelligence.

There is another reason why progress towards developmental scales of language has been slow. It is difficult to decide how speech should be collected. The speech emitted by anyone depends upon the situation in which it was evoked. For example, if you ask children to describe a colourful, crowded picture, they are likely to use a good many different adjectives. If you ask them to make up a story, they may use many more clauses. Now this means that speech collected in one situation may not be a representative sample of a child's linguistic repertoire. Of course, we can give the children a number of tasks during an interview which will tap a good selection of verbal skills. Even then, however, children respond differently to interviews. Some children are shy and give only a sketchy impression of their possible resources. Children also interpret tasks rather differently. Some children, when presented with a picture for description, will embark upon a complicated narrative; others will simply list items in the picture.

The members of the research unit devised a comprehensive interview. The children were given the opportunity to describe pictures, to tell stories, to explain games and the way toys worked and so forth. Interviewers were briefed to encourage children to say as much as they could. This speech was recorded and transcribed. The linguists of the research unit have, since then, been working on a system of analysis which may eventually make it possible to discriminate between children at different points on a developmental continuum. Just as tests of intelligence took a long time to be perfected, this system of linguistic analysis is a full-scale research project in itself and is still incomplete. The linguists' project was initiated at about the same time as the intervention programme and, thus, was not sufficiently advanced for us to use their findings.

Had there been available reliable measures of language development and skills, we would have used these both for initial tests to ensure comparability, and also for final testing to assess the effects of the programme.

Initially the children were given three tests of verbal and non-verbal intelligence before the programme started. One of these was used later as a basis for matching children from different experimental groups. This was done, since it could be argued that verbal skills are affected by intelligence. Furthermore, the programme might have affected differentially children scoring differently on these tests. It was important to obtain a good range of scores across all three groups.

The children were, in fact, given further tests of intelligence during the project. The comparisons between the first and later tests were made very complex by the initial variability between schools and groups. This analysis will be available in a separate, more technical publication. It is not being used for evaluation at this point. One general finding of interest here is that in the later tests at age 7 years children in both control groups of schools were showing a deterioration in performance. This is in line with Douglas's[17] finding of a similar deterioration in performance by children of this social class between the ages of 8 and 12.

Thus we could not use pure language tests, and we did not want to use tests of intelligence for evaluating the effects of the programme. Even without testing intelligence, one still prefers to use measures which have been standardized on a large population of subjects. It is then possible to assess the significance of differences observed between groups of children in terms of some more general standard. However, apart from the English Progress Test A2,[18] which is a standardized test of attainments, this could not be done. We concentrated on a different approach to evaluation.

We developed a number of tests in which the children were obliged to use language and in which we believed that performance would be enhanced by superior language skills. Some of these tests involved problem-solving, some learning, some of them simply probed the child's ability to code in language a particular experience. The tests were exploratory, since we do not know the characteristic performance of children of this age on such tasks. During the rest of this chapter we present these experiments, their results and the conclusions that we drew from them together with the results of the standardized attainment test. In designing the experiments, we argued that children with enhanced linguistic ability should give superior performances. Our reasoning here involved two stages. Firstly, that superior language skills would facilitate performance and, secondly, that E1 children would have superior language skills. If the first assumption were incorrect, we would not be able to demonstrate the truth of the second assumption.

We divided the children into groups in a way that would enable us to make a number of comparisons. This procedure was adopted for all the experiments but one. Firstly, we compared the performances of E1 children with those of one or both C group children. Secondly, we compared the performances of children scoring high, medium or low on the initial matching tests irrespective of experimental group. Thirdly, we compared the performance of girls with that of boys irrespective of experimental group and of initial score. In addition, we could take combinations of these comparisons, e.g. girls high on initial score with girls low on initial score. We call this kind of experimental procedure a factorial design. In some experiments there were additional factors for comparison which we shall describe in context.

We mentioned earlier that, owing to the mismatch in ability between children in E1 and C schools as a whole on initial tests, we had to use sub-samples of children for the experiments. We selected those children from an experimental group yielding a high average score, a medium average score and a low average score on the initial tests of verbal ability. Thus, the very high or very low scorers on initial tests who were contributing to mismatch were omitted for the experiments. It meant that, of course, this sub-sample of children was repeatedly tested.

One further point has to be made about the use of the two control groups. Ideally we should always have used children from both control groups for all the experiments. Unfortunately, there were limitations on the time we could spend testing. Where we tested both control groups, our prediction was always that the C2 group (the Hawthorne group) would be superior to the C1 group, due to enhanced motivation on the part of the teachers. When we had to limit ourselves to a comparison with one control group, we always selected the C2 children, since this would provide a more rigorous test of the programme. Let us turn to the experiments.

A problem-solving test using thematic materials

This experiment was carried out nine months after the programme had started.

The children had to select from a number of alternatives an appropriate picture to complete a series. This series made a little story and consisted of four pictures in all, but with one missing. The picture might be missing from any one of the four positions. Four of the five alternative pictures were closely relevant to the story series. For example, one picture was relevant for a position before the story begins, one was relevant for a position after the story ends, one was identical with a picture already exposed, and, of course, there was the correct choice picture. The fifth picture was totally irrelevant, containing no elements in common with the series. There were ten such problems to solve. Now, in this experiment we made an additional comparison. We had half our children, that is, half the children from each division made in terms of experimental group, initial ability and sex, describe all the pictures before choosing the missing item. The other half had only to choose the missing item without saying anything. We argued that here was a task where verbalization should help the child to solve the problem. Therefore, by comparing the groups who described the pictures with those who did not, we could test the validity of this argument. We also, of course, expected that children from the E1 groups of schools would do better than the controls, and that children of high initial ability would do better than children of low initial ability. In all we tested 72 children equally selected from E1 and C2 schools and further divided into equal groups of high, medium and low E.P.V.T. scorers of each sex.

Applying an analysis of variance to the results, what we found was that (1) there was no difference between the performance of children asked to verbalize and those who were not; (2) that children from E1 did not differ overall from those in C1; (3) that boys did not differ from girls; but (4) that children of different initial ability did indeed differ in performance, that is, that children scoring high on the initial E.P.V.T. test were better than children scoring low, significant at the ·001 level, with the medium scorers coming in between. However, if we took each level of initial ability separately, we found that of the medium group E1 were better than C1, significant at the ·05 level.

It is possible, then, that the differences due to initial ability were masking differences due to the programme. However, since we failed to demonstrate that describing the items, that is, using language overtly to solve the problems, significantly facilitated performance, we cannot regard this as a particularly good test of improved language skills. With this experiment we do not know whether the failure to obtain an overall difference between E1 and C1 groups was due to (*a*) lack of effects from the programme; (*b*) the fact that the programme had not been running long enough; (*c*) the finding that initial ability was a far more important determinant of superior performance; or (*d*) the fact that the test was not really one of improved linguistic skill. The results suggest that the latter two reasons are nearer the truth. The next experiment was a test of a rather different nature and provided us with a more satisfactory index of verbal skill.

A test of verbal facility and verbal learning

There is considerable interest, among psychologists, in the ability of children to learn verbal material. It is widely believed that a child's total verbal repertoire has important effects on this type of learning. One method of examining it is to present children with pairs of items, the first having to be associated with and linked to the second. For example, we may present him with pairs of pictures, a house and an apple, a flower and a tea-pot and so on; he then has to learn to respond with the word 'apple' when he sees the picture of a house and with 'tea-pot' when he sees the picture of a flower. He may be presented with a list of ten such pairs. The speed with which a child learns to correctly associate the second member of a pair with the first varies greatly. One way of enhancing his learning is to ask him to make up a little sentence containing the two picture words, e.g. 'the flower is next to the tea-pot'. If young children hear the two words in such a sentence while looking at the two pictures, they learn more quickly to associate them. This sentence construction, however, makes no difference to the learning speed of older children. One reason is probably that they covertly make up their own linking sentences when exposed to the pictures. Now, we considered it likely that our E1 children, then aged 6 – 9 to 7 – 3, would be more like older children of around 8 to 10 years in being readily able to make such linking sentences, and thereby be much quicker at learning such a list. We used eight pairs of pictures for the test.

First we ensured that the children could name the objects represented on each of the sixteen pictures. Then they were shown the pictures in pairs, and, after having been given three examples of sentences linking the two objects in a practice pair, they were asked to make a little sentence. When they had done this for each pair, the learning trials began. The children were shown the first picture and had to say what was the other member of the pair. If they didn't know it, it was shown to them. This continued until they would correctly anticipate all the items on two successive runs. The children were tested individually.

We chose 54 children for the experiment, selected equally from E1, C1 and C2 schools with an equal number of boys and girls. The children were also divided in terms of their E.P.V.T. scores into High, Medium and Low scorers, so that E.P.V.T. scores and sex were equally represented in all groups.

We examined the quality of the sentences produced in terms of the number of different verbs used by each child over the eight pairs. We found that the average number of different verbs produced by E1 children was considerably higher than those shown by C1 and C2 children. The difference was increasingly obvious the lower the E.P.V.T. scores, i.e. the greatest difference was between E1 and both control groups for the Low group. We also examined the number of trials needed for a child to reach the learning criterion and found that E1 needed fewer trials than either C1 or C2 children. Applying an analysis of variance to the results the differences between E1 and C1 and between E1 and C2 children on both measures were found to be significant beyond the ·01 level. Finally, the two measures were correlated and produced a coefficient of $-·36$ which was also significant beyond the 0·1 level.

What can we conclude from these results? Firstly, although up to the time at which this experiment was conducted no specific training in sentence production had been included in the language programme, E1 children produced more varied sentences than either of the control groups of children. Secondly, although there was nothing in the programme specifically aimed at improving performance in a simple learning situation such as paired-associate learning, at this age at least, by improving a child's verbal repertoire in general, we had increased his ability to produce a range of sentences; and this increased ability in turn facilitated his learning of the material. Finally, the significant negative correlation between the number of different verbs produced and trials to criterion, supports our contention that it was in fact the sentential linking of the items to be learnt which facilitated learning. This experiment is reported in greater detail elsewhere.[19]

A test of codability: Visual discrimination

The next experiment was a test of a rather different nature. It was an experiment on codability and was designed and carried out by W. P. Robinson and C. D. Creed.[20] We suggested earlier in this book that one aim of the language programme was to enable children to put into words finer distinctions, discriminations and qualifications. Codability in this context refers to the translation into verbal forms of experience internally felt or externally received through the senses. In other words, it is the attaching of verbal symbols to experience. We have already referred to a tradition of thinking among many psychologists, anthropologists and linguists that it is only through this verbal coding process that we are able to experience fine distinctions and differences between perceived objects and between our internal states of mind, moods and feelings. This view of the primary importance of language for determining the quality of our experience is implicit in the writings of Bernstein. The following experiment was designed to evaluate the effect of the programme on the child's coding ability.

The children were presented with pairs of pictures one at a time, the two members of a pair being identical for a limited number of deliberately introduced differences.

One member of a pair was shown first. The child was allowed to look at it for as long as he wished and was asked to report what was in the picture. Then, she was shown the second member of the pair and asked to point to the differences. When this had been done, the child had to say what the differences were. It was predicted that, as a result of participation in the language programme, E1 children would spend more time looking at the first picture of each pair, would notice more attributes and hence point to more differences between the members of each pair and would be better able to verbally code these differences than the control children. The scoring of verbalizations, that is, of the differences reported, was based on the degree of specificity adopted by the child. Simple statements of difference, e.g., 'they're different', or of recognition of the attribute, e.g., colour, were scored 0; statements indicating recognition of the attributes plus a statement of the value of the attribute in one picture, or a statement indicating recognition of both values of the attribute, e.g., 'That's red and this one's green', were scored 1. Of the thirty-two codable differences, eight were omissions, seven were differences of colour, seven were differences of shape or position, eight were differences in faces or clothes of persons portrayed, with one spelling and one number difference.

G

The experimenters tested a small sample of 24 girls aged between 7 and $7\frac{1}{2}$ equally selected from E1 and C2 schools and further divided into 4 high and 8 low E.P.V.T. scorers to each group. Results showed that there were no differences in time spent studying the first picture for any of the comparisons made. Differences in pointing, significant beyond the ·001 level, were obtained between high and low E.P.V.T. scorers in favour of the high group, but there was no E1 – C2 difference. A similar E.P.V.T. difference significant at the ·001 level in favour of high scorers was found for verbalization and, when differences in pointing were partialled out, E1 produced more efficient descriptions of differences than C1 significant beyond the ·05 level.

It seems clear from these results that this experimental technique for examining the relationship between children's perceptual discriminations and codability is a valuable one. However, since the sample of children tested in this experiment was small and since only girls participated as subjects with unequal numbers in the two E.P.V.T. groups, caution must be exercised in interpreting the results. It would be unwise to generalize from these results to the experimental population as a whole, though the significant E1 – C2 difference is suggestive.

A test of codability: Tactile discrimination

In describing the activities used in the language programme in Chapter 4, we mentioned the extensive use of variations on the I-Spy game, especially during the first two years of the project. The aim of these activities was to sharpen the discrimination of the children's perception of qualitative and quantitative differences between objects along dimensions of colour, shape, size, texture and so on, and to provide the children with a vocabulary for the expression of these differences. The previously-described experiment was one attempt to ascertain the value of this training.

A particular variation on the I-Spy game which was introduced for a time during the second year of the project consisted of a guessing game in which children had to identify objects described by another child who could feel them but not see them inside a box. At the end of the final year of the programme we designed an experiment to examine the effect of this and related activities concerned with the coding of tactile experience. At the time at which the children were tested no training of this kind had been carried out for more than a year.

The children were presented with pairs of cloth bags. Each bag contained a different object. For example, a piece of tree bark, a lump of sugar, a sponge, a tea-strainer and so on. The child had to put one hand in each bag and to describe to the experimenter as many differences between the two objects as he could feel. When the child had finished, the experimenter had to guess what the objects were. At no time until he had completed his description of the objects did the child see them, and the guessing of their identity was the task of the experimenter. A child's score consisted of the total number of tactile properties attributed to each of the twelve objects used. However, unlike the previous experiment, this did not take account of the *quality* of the child's verbalization. Examples of the verbalization produced are 'it's curved', 'it's got lots of little holes', 'it's bendable', 'it's like a fish shape', 'you can pull it apart', 'if you squeeze it, it stays in the same position as you put it', and 'it's heavier than the other one'.

We selected 90 children to participate in the experiment. Thirty were chosen from each of the experimental groups of schools (E1, C1 and C2) and were equally divided into boys and girls and into three E.P.V.T. groups, high, medium and low. The age range was 7–11 to 8–5 years.

An analysis of variance carried out on the results showed that E1 children made more tactile discriminations than either C1 or C2 children. This result was significant at the ·001 level in both cases. There was also an overall difference between E.P.V.T. groups significant at the ·05 level and attributable to a difference between high and low scorers significant at the ·025 level. There was no sex difference. These results were clearly very encouraging, since they suggested that at least in the area of tactile discrimination and codability the effects of the language programme were long-lasting.

A verbal concept sorting test

Among the tests of evaluation which we used, the following experiment was the closest of all to the language programme, both in terms of the time elapsed between training and testing and in terms of similarity of training and testing procedures. Earlier, we mentioned the difficulty encountered in educational research of selecting evaluation tests which are a fair measure of whatever new procedures or techniques are being tried out. At the most obvious level, items used in the training must not be used for evaluation. However, to decide what would constitute a specific coaching effect and what would constitute a more general transfer of skill effect is not always easy; it is especially difficult when attempting to estimate the effects of enhanced linguistic skill on cognitive processes. We considered the previously-described experiment on codability to be justified largely on grounds of the time-lapse between training and evaluation and of the expected generalization of an acquired vocabulary of touch to novel objects and new situations. The justification for the experiment we shall now describe was rather different.

From the fourth to the eighth term of the language programme the children were regularly required to form superordinate concepts by classifying various items under group names. The purposes of this activity were to sharpen the children's powers of discrimination by stressing the multiple attributes possessed by any object, to emphasize the matrix of possible relationships that one object can have with other objects, to provide them with a vocabulary for expressing superordination, and, incidentally, to enhance the children's short-term retention of verbally-transmitted material. This last effect was spontaneously reported by the project teachers shortly after the introduction of this activity. From learning to hold seven or eight exemplars and one non-exemplar of a concept simultaneously in mind before attaining the concept, there seemed to be a transfer of skill to other parts of the teaching curriculum. Whether this was due to enhanced attention to what was said rather than to enhanced retention, we are not able to say.

Because of the obvious importance of this activity for the cognitive and linguistic development of the children, we devised an experiment which, while close to the training itself, used items not previously encountered by the children. They were presented with groups of four words, three of which were examples of a concept, the other being a non-exemplar. For example, of the four words 'case, sink, bag, basket' only three are *portable* containers, although all four are containers. Similarly, of the four words, 'if, maybe, definitely, perhaps', three are expressions of possibility, the other of certainty. Twenty such groups of words and two practice groups were used, ranging in difficulty from simple concrete to highly abstract concepts.

The children were first required to say which of the four words was different from the other three and, secondly, to say what was the same about the three, that is, to provide the concept label. Since a child might have the concept but not the label, there were two scores: (i) the number of correct choice responses out of twenty, and (ii) the number of correct verbalizations of the concept. It was predicted that children who had had the language programme would make more correct choice responses and more correct concept verbalizations than children from either control group.

The test was given to a sample of 90 children at the end of the final term of the project. The children were equally selected from E1, C1 and C2 groups of schools, further divided into three ability groups (high, medium and low) on the basis of their E.P.V.T. scores, and with equal numbers of boys and girls. The children were aged 7 – 11 to 8 – 5 years at the time of testing and were all seen by the same researcher.

Applying an analysis of variance to the subjects' scores no significant differences were found on either measure between E1, C1 and C2 or between boys and girls, though E1 obtained a higher mean score than either C1 or C2 in both cases. There were significant differences on both measures between each of the E.P.V.T. groups, with high scorers doing better than medium scorers, who did better than low scorers. The difference between the two measures, that is, between correct choice responses and correct verbalizations of the concept, was calculated as a percentage loss of responses through verbalization. E1 children's scores changed less (17·19% loss) than C1 (25·12% loss) or C2 (24·41% loss). Our assumption that the items covered a range of difficulty was supported by the results. The number of children obtaining a correct choice response score on each item ranged from 88 to 23, and the number obtaining a correct concept verbalization score on each item ranged from 80 to 15. The curve for items in both cases was linear, though our own ranking of the items for difficulty prior to the experiment was not matched by the children's performance.

What could we conclude from this experiment? It is clear that the major effect of this test was to discriminate between children of different ability and that the relevant activities of the language programme had not had a sufficiently large impact on the children to produce a significant difference. A subsidiary X^2 analysis was carried out on the E1, C1 and C2 verbalization scores, since these had produced the larger differences between means, in order to take account of discrepancies between test items. We combined the frequencies of C1 and C2 correct verbalizations for each item separately and compared them with the frequencies of E1. For 17 out of the 20 test items the results were in favour of E1, for two there was no difference, and on the other the controls were superior. This gave a CR of 3·492 significant in favour of E1 at the ·0005 level. This meant that whilst there was no overall significant experimental group difference in total test scores, certain items, especially at the higher level of difficulty, discriminated between the groups in favour of E1. Had we raised the ceiling of this test by including items of greater difficulty or had we simply included more difficult and less simple items, we might well have produced a more obvious programme effect.

Two tests of verbal creativity

During the past fifteen years or so researchers in the field of educational psychology have shown increasing interest in creativity as a separate dimension of personality. Traditionally, intelligence as measured by I.Q. tests has been viewed as the major determinant of a child's academic performance and as a predictor of his achievement in adulthood. Creativity has either been ignored as being of limited importance or has been regarded as simply a facet of general intellectual ability. In other words, creativity has been subsumed under intelligence. However, there is at present considerable argument in the literature as to whether creativity is dependent upon or independent of general intelligence. Michael Wallach and Nathan Kogan[21] recently reviewed some of the major studies of creativity reported in the psychological literature, and observed that, contrary to current popular belief, most measures of creativity correlate more highly with measures of intelligence than they do among themselves. However, the same authors reported that they had developed tests which seemed to successfully isolate a creativity factor which was independent of intelligence. Their tests differed from those of other investigators not so much in content as in techniques of administration. They argued that creativity could be isolated as an independent factor when the tests were administered in relaxed 'non-test' like circumstances and when there was no temporal constraint, in other words children would produce creative responses only if the testing was unpaced and did not arouse anxiety.

However, Wallach and Kogan's sample consisted of 151 middle-class children aged 10 – 11 years. Since they did not report the range of scores obtained on the tests of intelligence that they used, it might well be the case that to obtain high scores on creativity tests a minimum degree of verbal maturity is a *necessary*, though not a sufficient condition. It may well have been the case that their middle-class children had all reached a sufficiently high degree of verbal maturity for creativity to become an independent factor. Since the authors established their high and low intelligence groups in terms of the sample under test and not in terms of norms for the population at large, it is possible that their sample was biased towards the higher regions of the intelligence scale.

Consequently, we decided to examine the performance of our

project children at the lower end of the intelligence scale on two tests of creativity. We considered that for these children aged 7 to 8 years high creativity scores would not be obtained, because they would not have reached a sufficiently high degree of verbal maturity for creativity to make an appearance. Thus a different combination of the two factors, age and verbal intelligence, to that used by Wallach and Kogan might well reveal a different relationship between creativity and intelligence. Furthermore, since the language programme had been aimed at improving the verbal skills and extending the verbal repertoire of the children, then, if it had been successful *and* if the preceding argument was sound, E1 low-verbal children would obtain higher creativity scores than low-verbal children in the control groups. The categorization of a child as 'low-verbal' referred to his score on the E.P.V.T. obtained before the onset of the language programme when the children were five years old. We made no predictions for the high- and medium-verbal children, except that, provided we could meet the testing conditions specified as necessary by Wallach and Kogan, we would not find any relationship between creativity and verbal ability in the medium to high range.

For both tests we examined the same sample of 90 children equally selected from E1, C1 and C2 schools and equally divided by sex into three ability groups (high, medium and low) on the basis of their initial E.P.V.T. scores. All children were tested by the same researcher with an interval of a fortnight between the two tests. It was not difficult to establish a relaxed atmosphere for testing the children. The researcher was well known to them and they were still young enough to treat any task as a game, so that there was no implication of evaluation in terms of a success-failure criterion. In fact, the eagerness of the children to be seen by the researcher during her visits to the schools considerably increased the time-cost of the experiments, since she had to see all children in the class, including non-sample children, on each occasion to avoid disappointing them and creating an impression of 'favouritism'. The children were all tested during the last month of the final term of the project when they were aged 7 – 11 to 8 – 5 years.

We turn now to the actual tests which were adapted by us from two of the several tests described by Wallach and Kogan.

Test 1: Instances

In this test the child was asked to generate as many instances of a verbally-specified class concept as possible. Specifically, the child had in turn to name (*a*) all the round things he could think of, (*b*) all the things that he could think of which will make a noise, (*c*) all the square things he could think of, and (*d*) all the things that he could think of that move on wheels. The child was given as much time as he wished for each item. The researcher exerted no pressure for speed, but rather encouraged the child to continue working on a given item for as long as he seemed to want to. Only when the child indicated that he had finished with a given item did the researcher turn to the next. The index of creativity used was the total number of responses (instances) produced across the four items. Wallach and Kogan used two indices in their study: (i) the total number of responses produced across all items, and (ii) the number of unique responses produced, a unique response for a given item being a response produced by only one child in the sample under test. However, since the two indices correlated very highly—unique responses tended to be produced at the end of the child's list, and the longer the list the greater the likelihood of unique responses—we settled for the first measure.

Test 2: Alternate uses

In the second test the child had to generate as many uses for a verbally-specified object as possible. Specifically, he had to tell the researcher (*a*) all the different ways he could use a newspaper, (*b*) all the different ways he could use a button and (*c*) all the different ways he could use a cork. The same testing conditions applied as in Test 1 and the index of creativity used was the total number of responses (uses) produced across the three items.

The results of both tests were subjected to an analysis of variance. In neither case was there a significant difference or significant interaction for any of the factors, nor were there significant differences between the E1 low-verbal group and the low-verbal control groups. In other words, whilst we failed to demonstrate any effect of the language programme on creativity at any level of ability, our results suggested that we had successfully replicated with younger children the finding of Wallach and Kogan that verbal creativity is independent of verbal intelligence. To ascertain that both tests were measuring the same thing, namely, creativity, we correlated the two sets of scores for all 90 subjects. This produced a coefficient of ·47 significant at the ·001 level. To investigate further the finding that there were no significant differences between groups of different ability, we separately correlated the scores on each of the tests with the subjects' E.P.V.T. scores, expecting a low non-significant correlation. The coefficients for E.P.V.T. and Instances and for E.P.V.T. and Uses were ·19 in both cases. This figure was not significant.

Whilst the reader unfamiliar with the psychologist's approach to creativity may be surprised to learn that such simple tests are used to measure a person's creativity, he must keep in mind the fact that only by pursuing the ideal of complete objectivity in assessment can we begin to understand what is involved in creativity. If the reader will simply consider how impossible it would be to arrive at objective, universally-agreed-upon criteria of creativity in painting, he will appreciate the reasons why psychologists have adopted such an approach.

Two tests for assessing sensitivity to physiognomic properties

Throughout the language programme we stressed the importance of sharpening the children's perception of emotion and interpersonal relations and extending their vocabulary for this area of experience. This emphasis was based on certain propositions contained in the theory of elaborated and restricted code. Bernstein maintains that the area of individual emotion and interpersonal relations is less adequately treated in the language of the restricted code user. One consequence of this is that the intentions and feelings of others will be taken for granted and language not be seen as a vehicle for exploration in this area.

The term 'physiognomic' refers to those properties of stimuli which are perceived in terms of affect and denoted emotional significance. It is possible to distinguish between such properties and purely physical attributes, which are usually referred to as geometric-technical. Presumably any visual stimulus can evoke physiognomic or geometric-technical responses. In fact, investigators have mainly examined responses to abstract visual stimuli, such as lines, patterns, colour arrangements and so on which do not possess an intrinsic physiognomic property. Nevertheless, a jagged line for many subjects denotes anger, a smooth one does not. There is considerable consensus among adult subjects in making such judgements.

As part of their study of creativity which we mentioned earlier Wallach and Kogan investigated the sensitivity of their subjects to physiognomic properties. They used abstract visual patterns as well as a series of photographed stick figures which had been developed by Professor Sarbin of Berkeley in work on role perception. These figures can reasonably evoke either physiognomic interpretations or descriptions in terms of the physical properties. For all tests Wallach and Kogan found that children high in both creativity and in intelligence produced more physiognomic interpretations. Since part of the language programme had been concerned with enhancing the sensitivity of the children to emotion and interpersonal relations and providing a vocabulary for expressing these perceptions, we considered that the stick figures would provide a reasonable test of sensitivity. We devised two tests to this effect.

Test 1: Single stick figures

For the first test the children were presented singly with twenty photographs of different single stick figures, kindly lent by Professor Sarbin for this experiment, and were asked to tell the researcher everything they could about them. The figures were all in different postures. The child's responses were independently coded by two judges into three categories: (1) High: any response which attributed emotion, motivation, volition or mood to a stick figure, e.g. 'He's sad/disappointed/wants to go home, etc.'; (2) Medium: any response describing action states, e.g. 'He's leaning against a door', or attributing a cognitive state to a stick figure, e.g. 'He's thinking', or involving a simile, e.g. 'He's like a rabbit coming out of its hole'; and (3) Low: any atomistic or fragmentary response describing parts of the figure separately, e.g. 'His legs are bent and his hands are above his head'. If a stick figure received a response covering more than one category, e.g. 'He's jumping up and down because he's happy', it was assigned to the higher category of the two.

Test 2: Related stick figures

Since the first test excluded statements of an interpersonal nature, we produced 12 pictures showing pairs of stick figures related to each other through posture and gesture, e.g. offering, comforting, greeting, rejecting, etc. Again the children were presented with the pictures one at a time and asked to tell everything they could about them. The responses were independently coded by two judges into three categories: (1) High: any responses describing the figures directly in terms of an affective relationship with each other, e.g. 'He's angry with him'; 'He's saying "Don't be sad, I didn't mean to hit you"'; (2) Medium: any response describing the figures as being in relation to each other but without mentioning any affective or motivational factor, e.g. 'He's following/hitting/looking away from the other one'; and (3) Low: where there was no specification of a relationship, and where the figures were described in isolation either wholly or in parts. Where a response covered more than one category it was assigned to the higher of the two.

For both tests we examined the same sample of 90 children equally selected from E1, C1 and C2 schools and equally divided by sex into three ability groups (high, medium and low) on the basis of their initial E.P.V.T. scores. The children were all tested during the first half of the final term of the project when they were aged 7 – 9 to 8 – 3 years. The administration of the two tests by the same researcher was separated by an interval of a fortnight.

We expected that on both tests E1 children would produce more responses coded as High than either of the control groups of children, thus indicating an increased sensitivity to physiognomic properties attributable to the language programme. We applied an analysis of variance to the results of each test. On Test 1 there were no significant differences between E1, C1 and C2 or between boys and girls, though the differences were in the expected direction, with E1 having a higher mean score than C1 or C2. There was a difference significant at the ·001 level between the E.P.V.T. groups, which upon further analysis was found to be due to a difference between the High and Medium groups significant at the ·025 level and between the High and Low groups significant at the ·001 level. There was no difference between the Medium and Low groups. There were no significant interactions. On Test 2 there were no overall significant differences between E1, C1 and C2 or between boys and girls, though again the differences were in the expected direction, with E1 having a higher mean score than C1 or C2. There was an E.P.V.T. group difference significant at the ·05 level. However, the picture was complicated by interactions between experimental groups and sex and between E.P.V.T. groups and sex significant at the ·05 and ·025 levels respectively. What this meant was that in the case of the first interaction E1 girls obtained higher scores than C1 or C2 girls, but the position was reversed, though to a lesser extent, for boys. In the case of the second interaction E1 High and Low E.P.V.T. children obtained higher scores than their counterparts in either C1 or C2, but the position was reversed for the Medium groups. We are not able to suggest any reason for these interaction effects, which were not found in either Test 1 or in any of the other experiments which we have reported.

The results then from the point of view of the language programme were disappointing. Did it mean that we had failed to have any effect on the children in one of our major areas of focus? Or did it mean that we had simply failed to find a suitable measure of the effect? Further examination of the responses suggested that the latter reason was nearer the truth. The reader will recall that in addition to activities aimed at sharpening the children's sensitivity to affect and interpersonal events, there were many activities whose aim was to train the children to attend to fine detail, to make fine discriminations and offer exact and precise descriptions of objects and events. What we found was that a small number of E1 children, mainly boys, seemed to have given precise, meticulous descriptions of the stick figures at the expense of holistic, relational responses. For example, they specified the exact location of each arm and each leg in relation to the body, whether the head was turned to the left or right, and whether a foot seemed to be raised off the ground. These and many similar responses were given by these E1 children, responses that in the context of this experiment were coded as Low and seemed almost pedantic in their exactitude, but which, in other contexts, might be extremely important. We seemed to have obtained a transfer of training effect that in this particular test situation was inappropriate from the researcher's viewpoint but, given the nature of the instructions to the children, was not perhaps altogether so surprising. We had not wished to give the children a set to produce High responses but as a result had inadvertently given some E1 children a set to produce Low responses.

In conclusion, then, we have shown in a number of experiments that the language programme has had an effect upon the children. We have shown (1) that there has been an improvement in their ability to generate sentences which in turn had an effect on performance in a simple learning task; (2) that they are able both to make and code finer discriminations among objects presented visually or tactually; and (3) in keeping with this there has been an effect on their ability to use superordination which is an important prerequisite for abstract thinking. Although each of these experiments reflects improvements in very specific skills, we would argue that such skills are basic to most aspects of superior educational performance.

In other experiments we have failed to demonstrate an effect due to the language programme, though the differences were usually in the right direction and, in the case of problem solving, were significant for a particular ability group. We have already outlined the difficulty encountered by any researcher of having to decide whether failure to obtain an effect experimentally is due to lack of an effect or to limitations in the experiment itself.

Differences in the control of others*

One of the major goals of the language programme was an enhance-
ment of the children's powers of discrimination. To this end, much
of the material developed for the programme encouraged the children to become aware of a range of alternatives from which they
could choose. Many of the picture stories encouraged the children
to explore both inter- and intra-personal relationships. The dramatic
play situations placed customary roles, like those of the aged and
the policeman, in unusual contexts. This material we hoped would
encourage the child to consider questions of intention, motivation
and consequence, and to become more reflective about various
types of social relationships. A remarkable opportunity arose to
evaluate, if only very indirectly, a possible consequence of this
attempted extension of the children's perceptions of others.

Before the children went to school for the first time a tape-
recorded interview took place with the mothers. During this interview the mothers were asked six hypothetical questions about how
they would control their child. Two and a half years later when the
children were commencing their first term in the junior school, the
six questions in a slightly modified form were given to the children
(see Appendix 3 for the questions). This provided us with a unique
opportunity to examine whether the programme had in any way
affected the children's perception of the control of others. We could
argue that if there was no difference between the mothers of the
children in the E1 and C2 schools in the way they said they controlled their children, no difference in the family's social class
position, and no difference in the mean I.Q. of the children in the
two groups of schools, then if we found differences in the control
styles of the children we would have a very plausible reason for
attributing the difference to aspects of the language programme.

Miss Jenny Cook developed an analysis of maternal and child
control styles which will be fully reported in a future Sociological
Research Unit Monograph. Miss Cook distinguishes five control
styles. Our analysis here is carried out using only three of these
styles, Punishing, Firmness and Mediating, because, as we expected,
the children offered too few responses on the remaining two styles,
Affective and Pure Reasoning. A full description of the Punishing,
Firmness and Mediating styles are given in Appendix 3. Here we
will only describe them briefly. A Punishing style is where some
very *coercive* approach is used. Firmness is less coercive than Punish-

* We are grateful to Jenny Cook, W. Brandis and J. Goldberg for this
summary of their more detailed analysis which forms Appendix 3.

ing but still involves little more than a statement of *constraint*. The Mediating style is much more complex. Here the child is moving away from simple coercion and constraint and is showing some awareness of intentions which influences how he sees a misdemeanour, and some awareness of the importance of concessions in the control of others. We were very interested in whether the E1 children would use more mediating styles than the children in the C2 group. (Details of the sample used in this enquiry will be found in Appendix 3.)

We found that there was *no* significant difference between the 42 children in the E1 group and the 42 children in the C2 group in the frequency of Punishing and Firmness styles. However, the E1 children offered 92 Mediating styles whereas the C2 children offered 68 such styles. An analysis of variance shows that this difference is statistically significant at the ·05 level. Thus E1 children offered significantly more of the complex Mediating control style response than did the C2 children.

We also found that there were no significant differences between the control styles of the mothers of the children in the E1 and C2 schools, no significant differences in their social class position and no significant differences between the mean I.Q. of the children in the two groups of schools. It is also the case that we have good reason to believe that the teachers of the children did not differ in the way they controlled the children.

We therefore suggest that it is reasonable to argue that the language programme indirectly affected the E1 children's reported perceptions of the control of others, but we feel that more extensive research is needed into the relationships between speech forms and social control.

We have also a more extensive measure of any differential effects of the home background of the children upon their subsequent achievement.

An Index of Communication and Control was constructed by W. Brandis.[23] It is based upon an interview with all the mothers in the sample (with the exception of the mothers of the C1 children) which took place before the children entered the infant school.

The Index assesses:
(1) The degree to which mothers were likely to take up the child's attempts to interact verbally with the mother in a series of different controls.
(2) The degree to which mothers were likely to evade or avoid answering difficult questions put to them by their children.
(3) The degree to which mothers were likely to use coercive methods of control.

(4) The degree to which mothers were likely to explain to the child why they wanted a change in his behaviour.

(5) The emphasis the mothers placed upon the general explorative use of toys.

Index scores range from 40 to 160. We have found that the score on this Index relates very strongly to the child's W.I.S.C. score, to the mother's attitude to teachers, to her understanding of the educational process, to the child's teacher's estimate of both the brightness of the child and the child's future educational career.[24] It thus provides us with a global estimate of the family environment as this may influence the child at school.

We give below the average Index score of the mothers of the children who remained in the sample at the commencement of the first year of the Junior school. The mothers of the children in the C1 schools are not included as, in keeping with the requirements of the experimental design, they did not receive the full maternal interview. The numbers are slightly less than the number of children who received the E.P.T., because some of the tape recordings of the maternal interview were of too poor quality to transcribe.

Index of Communication and Control

School	Index Score	N
11	97·2	15
12	107·3	16
13	104·8	15
E1	103·2	46
21	98·2	14
22	108·7	15
23	104·5	13
C2	103·9	42
Total	103·5	88

The above figures indicate that there is *no* difference between the educational quality of homes of the E1 and C2 children, as this is reflected in the score on the Index of Communication and

Control obtained just *before* the children went to school. It could be argued that the educational quality of the home changed across the three years of the child's school life. However, as against this possibility, we have found high correlations between the score on the Index of Communication and Control and measures of the educational quality of the home obtained through the second interview of the mother when the child entered the Junior school.

Thus we have some evidence that the improvement of the children in the E1 schools does not arise out of the superior educational quality of their homes.

The English progress test A2*

We turn finally to the standardized test of attainment mentioned earlier in the chapter which was administered at the end of the third year. This was the final evaluation carried out in the research. The English Progress Test A2,[22] which we shall refer to hereafter simply as the EPT, is intended for children 7 and 8 years old and consists of 42 questions grouped into 10 sections, each testing a specific language skill. The child has to read the question and to write down the answer, so minimal literacy is a necessary condition for obtaining a score. The child's raw score, which is simply the total number of right answers, is converted to an age-standardized score with a mean of 100 and standard deviation of 15.

This test, which became available shortly before the project was completed, was ideally suited to our needs; firstly, because it had been recently standardized on an extremely large population of nearly 5,000 children; secondly, because it could be administered simultaneously to all children in a class by the class teacher; and thirdly, because it sampled a variety of language skills which curriculum English aims at developing, and so provided an excellent test of the possible transfer effects of the primarily oral language activities of the programme to written English.

We were naturally very keen to examine the performance of the children in our sample in the light of standardized data; to put it simply, how well our children performed on a test of English compared with children of the same age in the population. Consequently, the procedure we adopted was somewhat different from that used in the experiments reported earlier. We gave the EPT to all children remaining in the project schools, with the exception of one of the

_____
* We are grateful to W. Brandis for this summary of the main analysis which appears as Appendix 2.

C1 schools. The children in this school were not tested at the request of the head teacher, who had planned a full programme of activities for the end of term and who did not feel he could fit in any more testing. This gave us 133 children in eight schools. It also presented us with an opportunity of looking at differences between schools as well as between groups of schools.

It was decided to look at the incidence of low, medium and high scorers in E1 compared with the combined control schools (C1 and C2). A low score was counted as 85 and below, that is, any score more than one standard deviation below the mean; a medium score was counted as 86 to 114; and a high score as 115 and above, that is, any score more than one standard deviation above the mean. There was very little difference between E1, C1 and C2 in the overall mean scores. The following table sets out the distributions.

TABLE A *Frequency (proportion) of low, medium, and high EPT scorers in sample schools*

	Low: 85 or less	Mid: 86-114	High: 115 or more	Total
1 *E1 Schools*				
A	2 (·13)	12 (·80)	1 (·01)	15 (1·00)
B	1 (·06)	14 (·82)	2 (·12)	17 (1·00)
C	0 (·00)	14 (·78)	4 (·22)	18 (1·00)
Total	3 (·06)	40 (·80)	7 (·14)	50 (1·00)
2 *C2 Schools*				
D	9 (·60)	6 (·40)	0 (·00)	15 (1·00)
E	4 (·24)	10 (·59)	3 (·18)	17 (1·00)
F	5 (·29)	10 (·59)	2 (·12)	17 (1·00)
Total	18 (·37)	26 (·53)	5 (·10)	49 (1·00)
3 *C1 Schools*				
G	3 (·25)	8 (·67)	1 (·08)	12 (1·00)
H	(EPT not administered)			
I	6 (·27)	16 (·73)	0 (·00)	22 (1·00)
TOTAL	9 (·26)	24 (·71)	1 (·03)	34 (1·00)
GRAND TOTAL	30 (·23)	90 (·68)	13 (·10)	133 (1·00)

H

We find that only three children out of 50 in the E1 group obtain scores of 85 or below, whereas 27 children out of 83 children in C1 and C2 obtain scores of 85 or below. This difference is significant at the ·001 level. Even when we remove the school in C2 from the calculation because of the abnormally high incidence of low-scoring children, we find that we still have 18 children out of 68 children in C1 and C2 who are low scorers. This difference is significant at the ·01 level. The proportion of low EPT scorers in the non-E1 schools is higher than in the general population (p = <·05), whereas *the proportion of low EPT scorers in the E1 group is significantly lower than in the general population* (p = <·05).

This clearly represents a major difference between the E1 and non-E1 schools. We were concerned with examining whether the pattern of low EPT scores reflected the pattern of low WISC scores. (The children were given the WISC when they were aged 7 years.) As the Scottish revision of the WISC tends to yield higher scores than would be expected given a mean of 100, we decided to set low scoring on the WISC at 90 rather than 85. The following table sets out the number of children who score low on the EPT and the number of children in each school who score low on the WISC. The figures in brackets refer to the *proportion* of children in each school who score low on the EPT and who score low on the WISC.

TABLE B *Frequency (proportion) of low EPT and low WISC scorers in sample schools*

	Low EPT: 85 or less	Low WISC: 90 or less	Difference in proportions	n
1 E1 Schools				
A	2 (·13)	2 (·13)	·00	15
B	1 (·06)	1 (·06)	·00	17
C	0 (·00)	2 (·11)	−·11	18
Total	3 (·06)	5 (·10)	−·04	50
2 C2 Schools				
D	9 (·60)	3 (·20)	+·40	15
E	4 (·24)	2 (·12)	+·12	17
F	5 (·29)	1 (·06)	+·24	17
Total	18 (·37)	6 (·12)	+·24	49

3 *Cl Schools*

G	3 (·25)	4 (·33)	−·08	12
I	6 (·27)	9 (·41)	−·14	22
Total	9 (·26)	13 (·38)	−·12	34
GRAND TOTAL	30 (·23)	24 (·18)	+·05	133

An analysis of variance of repeated measures shows that the overall pattern of low EPT scoring does *not* reflect the overall pattern of low WISC scores ($p = <·001$). This is because of the large difference in the proportion of C2 children who score low on the EPT (·37) compared with the proportion who scored low on the WISC (·12). It appears that intervention of any kind (e.g. Hawthorne effect) reduces the incidence of low WISC scores *but it requires a language programme to reduce the incidence of low EPT scores.* This conclusion is in no way affected by the pattern of low EPVT scoring at the age of five; nor is it in any way a product of the arbitrary selection of cut-off points for the low categories.

We shall now look at the West Indian children in our sample. The following table sets out the distribution of the 11 West Indian children in the schools and it shows the mean EPVT scores, the mean WISC scores and the mean EPT scores for these children.

TABLE c *Distribution of the West Indian sample by school, with mean EPVT, WISC, and EPT scores*

	n	Mean EPVT	Mean WISC	Mean EPT
School B	3	82·3	88·7	88·7
School C	3	88·3	97·7	104·0
Total E1	6	85·3	93·2	96·3
School E (C1)	5	86·4	90·4	84·0
GRAND TOTAL	11	85·8	91·9	90·7

A similar analysis was carried out on these scores as was carried out on the low scoring English children. When we take into account the WISC scores of the children we find that the difference between the mean EPT scores of the West Indian children in E1 (96) is significantly higher ($p = <·05$) than the mean EPT scores of the West Indian children in the non-E1 school (84). This difference is still significant when we control for the initial EPVT scores of the children at five years of age.

Conclusion

Our conclusions are straightforward.
(1)   It is clearly the case that the language programme has greatly reduced the incidence of low-scoring children on the English Progress Test.
(2)   It is also the case that a language programme not specifically designed for West Indian children has increased their scores on the English Progress Test *relative* to their scores on the WISC.

Summary of the Evaluation of the Language Programme

Conclusion

We shall now list the results of the evaluation studies.
(1)   On all tests with the exception of the second of the two tests of verbal creativity the mean scores of the E1 children were higher than the mean scores of the C1 and C2 children.
(2)   On the paired associative learning test, which is a test of verbal facility and verbal learning, the E1 children produced significantly more varied sentences and learned the tasks more quickly than the children in the C1 and C2 groups. It seems that the language programme, by improving the child's language repertoire in general, had increased the children's ability to produce a range of sentences which in turn facilitated the specific learning required by this test.
(3)   There was a suggestive significant difference, albeit on a small sample of girls, that the E1 girls were better able to realize linguistically differences between items in sets of pictures.
(4)   When the children were seven years of age the children in the total sample answered the same questions about how they would deal with problems of the control of children which were put to their mothers. We found that the children in the E1 group used a mediating control style significantly more often than the C2 children. The greater frequency of a mediating control style indicates that the E1 children were relying less upon assertions of power and authority and were using more

often a flexible form of control involving some perception of the point of view of the controller and the controlled, some idea of the consequences of the act for the child or some other person, and the ability to modify the form of the social relationship through the use of concession strategies. This result cannot be attributed to either the sex or I.Q. of the child or to the control styles of the parents or teachers. Thus, the greater frequent use of mediating control styles can be attributed to aspects of the language programme and the social relationships and meanings which it made available.

(5) At the end of the final year of the project E1 children were significantly better than C1 and C2 children in their ability to discriminate verbally attributes of objects which they could feel but not see.

(6) At the end of the final year of the project E1 children were significantly better than C1 and C2 children at mastering the *more* difficult problems on a verbal concept sorting test, despite the fact that there was no overall significant difference in the mean scores between E1 and C1 and C2 children.

(7) At the end of the final year of the project there was a highly significant difference between the children in the E1 schools who scored below 85 on an English Progress Test (E.P.T.) and the number of children who scored low on this test in the C1 and C2 group. This result holds good when we control for the W.I.S.C. I.Q.s of the children. There were very many more children who scored *low* on this test in the C1 and C2 group than children in the E1 group. It is also the case that the West Indian children in the E1 group achieved a significantly higher *mean* score on the E.P.T. than West Indian children in the C1 and C2 group. This result holds good when we take into account the measured ability of the West Indian children.

(8) There is evidence that the programme benefited the less able child:

(a) On the paired associative learning task children with *low* E.P.V.T. scores produced more varied sentences and needed fewer trials to learn the task than did children with low E.P.V.T. scores in the C1 and C2 group.

(b) On the physiognomic test where the children had to talk about stick figures, children who scored low on the E.P.V.T. obtained more responses which indicated an awareness of affective and motivational aspects of the relationships between the figures than did children who scored low on the E.P.V.T. in C1 and C2 groups.

    (c)   There were many fewer children who obtained low scores on the E.P.T. than in the C1 and C2 groups.

(9)   There are suggestions which will require more analysis that children in the control groups suffered a decrement in their measured ability scores between the ages of five and seven years of age. This does not seem to be the case for the children in the E1 group.

There were no *over-all* significant differences between the E1 and C1 and C2 groups on the physiognomic and creativity tests.

We would suggest then that the language programme in total benefited the E1 children and in particular the children who were or who might have been placed in low ability groups. In addition perhaps we should point out that the notable discrepancy between the W.I.S.C. and E.P.T. scores may be an indication of what could be done given more time and resources.

Chapter 8   A Spot of Revolution

At this point we can return to one or two questions rather superficially discussed earlier. In Chapter 2 we mentioned that the children in the sample as a whole, more especially the E1 children, produced better performances on verbal tests than had been predicted. Their scores were slightly above the population norms. How would this fact tally with the thesis that children of this social class are linguistically restricted? We also presented in the same chapter evidence from another source that older children in this area are performing below average, particularly on verbal tests. This latter finding suggests, as in Douglas's study,[23] that some deterioration sets in with children of this social class after they enter junior school at eight. To return to the first point, we must remember that tests of vocabulary are not designed to measure the features of restricted code that Bernstein has described. Restricted code is language confined to a narrow range of social functions. Of course, one would expect tests of vocabulary to measure this restriction to some extent. On the other hand, absence of extreme deficiency here would not be sufficient to imply absence of restricted language in general. We feel that the selection of children in this area, in terms of social class indices, was a reasonable one, although children from another part of the borough, not included in the project, had scores nearer to the level that we had predicted.

The infant teaching specialist may be troubled by a rather different question. Traditional infant education for the last thirty years or so has stressed the importance of activity and exploration as a prerequisite for learning. Children spend a fair amount of time building, painting and playing. This approach is colloquially known as the 'play-way'. Now the emphasis in our programme has been on verbal formulation, on acquiring abstract concepts and strictly non-physical activity. We will not launch into a discussion of the quantitative and qualitative merits of the 'play-way'—we do not hold them in doubt. In the United States, however, this issue has

raised some sharp controversies. It is worth mentioning them here
to clarify our own recommendations. Enrichment programmes in
the States are usually carried out for disadvantaged children at pre-
school level (compulsory schooling starts a little later there). These
pre-schools are designed solely for this purpose, and teachers are
specially trained. Thus, there are no constraints on what may be
included in the programme. Now, until recently, these pre-schools
were set up along the same lines as nursery schools for more fortunate children. The emphasis was on providing a rich and
stimulating environment, freedom to explore and discover, and
encouragement towards individual self-expression. All this was
somewhat intensified for disadvantaged children, since the assumption made was that the home environment of such children would
be severely limited and impoverished. Two educationalists, Carl
Bereiter and Siegfried Engelmann, initiated an enrichment project
in sharp contrast to the policy of such pre-schools.[24] They stressed
that, for the disadvantaged child to reach a parity with his privi-
leged counterpart, he needs to progress at a faster rate. He has
already fallen behind developmentally, and, therefore, the same
type of experiences as normal children have will be inadequate.
This point can hardly be argued. At this point we must contrast
the disadvantaged child of the urban slum in America with the
lower working-class child here. The former is clearly much further
behind developmentally. They suggested, however, that there was
no evidence that the environment of disadvantaged children was
unstimulating or lacked opportunities for exploration and discovery.
They argued that the main deficiencies in this environment, as
opposed to the middle-class home, are the encouragement to be
attentive rather than distractable and the orientation towards post-
poned gratification and achievement. Demands which are made
once school begins. Above all, of course, they argued that the
linguistic environment of such children is hopelessly inadequate to
meet the demands of education. They cited in their book, *Teaching
Disadvantaged Children in the Pre-school*, a number of projects,
run in the traditional way, where initial improvements had been
shown to be short-lived, and advanced the foregoing argument in
explanation of these results. Accordingly, they initiated a pre-school
project, on academic, perhaps rather forbidding lines. This included
language training as well as other activities. Some part of each day
for these children was devoted to non-motoric intensive drills, conducted in an atmosphere more rigorous and less permissive than
present educational philosophy has recommended.

The situation within which our project was carried out was
entirely different. We had neither the intention nor wish to interfere

with prevailing infant school practice. We agreed with the proposition, however, that it was not necessary to provide the children in our sample with an even 'richer' environment than is already present in the school. Our effort centred around the argument that the existing activities of the children both at home and at school could be more closely linked to explicit language use. The Bereiter and Engelmann view is that certain aspects of language, ranging from rigorous attention to speech to the encouragement of careful and even more complex formulation, are the vital factors for disadvantaged children. We are in agreement with this. Where we produced procedures which might appear 'drill-like', these skills were linked to specific contextual requirements and real situations. It is the more rigorous cognitive demands made on the middle-class child at home which are responsible for his more flexible and varied use of language—and it was these demands that we tried to 'stage-manage' in the classroom.

The crucial point, of course, is whether there is time in the normal school day for both the optimal amount of play-way and for language-enrichment activities. We had difficulty in fitting in our twenty minutes per day—which was probably very inadequate. It is likely that to accommodate a programme for large periods, some other activities would have to be curtailed. However, as we have stressed here and in an earlier chapter, it is possible for the teacher to use the 'play-way' context for encouraging the type of verbal interaction which we believe to be important.

One further point is relevant to this discussion. When the child leaves the infant school for a separate junior department, there is frequently an abrupt change in approach. Education, even in the first junior class, is often on a much more formal basis. This change requires considerable adaptation on the part of children emerging from infant school. It could be argued that the demands arising out of this change fall more heavily on the child with inappropriate language. Indeed, it may be that the deterioration already referred to begins at this stage. To respond to teaching increasingly mediated through language the child must be equipped to meet the demands implied.

We can take the argument further. Even if junior schools changed in orientation, becoming more activity-oriented, as many people would recommend, at some point complex verbal skills are bound to become essential. It is probably at this point of transition (whenever it occurs) that the lower working-class child becomes dimly aware that there are two distinct worlds. In the world of home, immediate situations and physical reality take precedence. Language is barely separated from its situational referents. In the world of school, abstract considerations and remote goals are the order of the day. He is likely to find the latter of diminishing interest, since it demands exactly those skills that he lacks. We would predict that many of the lower working-class children who excel in natural sciences and technology must find themselves handicapped by inadequate verbal skills. They will be exceptional indeed if they triumph in such discursive areas as the social sciences or the fine Arts. We would certainly argue that unless these children acquire a flexible, competent use of spoken language, a real vehicle for individual expression, the demands of the average English syllabus from junior school onwards will not be met.

Is this period which we chose for intervention the correct one? We chose the first two years of formal school as our experimental period strictly for experimental reasons. There may be a 'close-season' for the modification of language skills. It is true that the natural sequence of language development has distinct regularities—with age-ranges across a population similar to such other activities as sitting-up or walking. However, apart from a widespread belief that a *second* language can be best acquired only very early in life, there is little evidence that one's language habits can or cannot be modified and extended at any time. Yet we all know of individuals who have broken through the barriers of lower working-class life and school to become, not engineers and physicists, but writers, sociologists and philosophers. If there were state nursery schools, there would be powerful arguments for starting special language programmes in them as early as possible. But why should there be an upper limit to this kind of focus? We would argue that the changing requirements of education made through the school demand continued emphasis on help in spoken language for those children who need it. The particular content of the programme we have presented was designed for children of the ages encompassed during the experiment. Yet many of the basic ideas and situations could be equally, if not more, relevant for older children. They would certainly be easier to manage. As children grow older they have more experience in more different individual areas that can be communicated to others; they have closer contact with a complex adult world. There seems no possible reason to recommend that special work on speech should occur in a circumscribed period as in our experiment, with the pious hope that it will have life-long effects. English is a tough subject at the lower end of the average secondary school. The basic reason is that children are being asked to manipulate written language, to meet demands which are rarely made on them outside the context of the English lesson. Had school from the beginning been a place where demands and occasions for precise and flexible verbal behaviour were customary, the uses of literacy would not seem quite so alien.

There is a dilemma which besets educational research (or any other research involving human beings). We are reluctant to introduce large-scale or drastic changes in teaching methods and curricula without a fair degree of confidence that they will be beneficial. On the other hand, it is difficult to discover whether or not they will be beneficial, unless they are applied intensively on a large scale. In our project we were reluctant to demand more time for our programme, yet we feel that the time allowed was insufficient to have lasting effects. A number of solutions are available, although we had at the time only a choice of two. One solution might have been to carry out a small, rigorously-controlled experiment in optimal but unnatural conditions. For example, we might have carried out language training on children in residential nurseries. In this case, we would have had unlimited time (as long as we didn't bore the children to death), specially trained teachers with nothing else to do, and only a small sample for extensive, carefully-timed pre- and post-testing. The advantage of this method is that one can confidently assess the effects of one's training procedures. On the other hand, one has no idea whether these procedures will be flexible or useful in the context for which they are intended—the infant school classroom. The alternative solution, which we adopted, was to carry out the experiment in the 'field'. We evolved, by a process of natural selection, the most feasible activities which teachers could carry out under any conditions. However, the disadvantages of this alternative have been dwelt on at length and culminate in the extreme problem of evaluation. However, we do know that the programme can be conducted in the classroom. This point is a very important one for teachers and heads who do not take kindly to specialists from other fields, making suggestions which are wildly difficult to carry out.

The main dilemma centred around this problem of time. We could not legitimately ask for more than 20 minutes per day without risking basic skills, or pre-basic skill activities, or play-way activities. Our programme was twenty minutes per day, one hour and forty minutes per week. If the programme had been concerned with some highly specific skill like knitting, or map-drawing, this time limit might have been less serious; the amount of interference from extra-programme activities would have been minimal. Our twenty minutes of 'elaborated code' was set in perhaps six or eight hours per day of language totally different in function. Of course, we tried (as described in Chapter 3) to orient the teachers towards developing the language medium throughout the day in conjunction with other work. However, we have no reliable way of finding out how far this was done.

The summary of the evaluation studies shows what has and has not been accomplished. Where experimental tests showed no difference between E1 and C children, we cannot know whether this was because (*a*) the activities in the programme had been ineffectual, (*b*) whether the time allowed was insufficient for them to be effective, or (*c*) because the tests themselves were not valid measures of the improvement predicted.

The statistical analysis of data from standardized tests of intelligence has to be presented later in a more technical publication, likewise the linguistic analysis. If our suspicions that the intelligence tests show the beginning of a deterioration in performance by C school children only are confirmed, this would also cast an encouraging light on the programme effects.

Let us, at this point, return to the more general but very basic questions discussed in the first chapter. Inappropriate language skills are among the several factors which account for educational underachievement among lower working-class children. We believe that it ranks high among these causative factors, but we do not know how high. This alone, however, is one justification for recommending special language programmes for the children who need them. It is not the only one. Real participation and power in social and political life implies the ability to manipulate the agencies which belong to everyone—from schools to unions, from local government offices to universities.

One of Bernstein's major propositions has been that the use of a restricted form of language arises within a particular social context and has a peculiarly social function. This form of language is at variance with the language required in education, given the present form, content and criteria used by the school. This means that, even, or perhaps especially, with the acquisition of a second form of language, certain children will have to operate in two worlds. One might question the value of equipping children with forms of speech, and concomitant attitudes and frames of reference, which will alienate them from the familial and neighbourhood environment. The following quotation is taken from an article by Brian Jackson who emerged from a lower working-class family to take First Class Honours in English at Cambridge:

Certainly, as it stands, education and its world of words is not
an extension of, but an exit from, the working class family.
Some may move back and forth, switching identities easily.
But when I once spoke to a group of former working class

children, many of them commonly mentioned an 'external' kind
of feeling as if they were looking in on something. . . . One of
the men I spoke to said: 'I feel more akin with them when
we're silent. I can get on with them better when we walk
silent together. It's when we start talking that we notice the
difference.'[25]

The message of this article was that the peculiar solidarity of
working-class family life with its excessive demands for conformity
is adapted to protect its members from the harsh contingencies by
which it is threatened. To move into another world of greater
physical but less psychological security is uncomfortable. Bernstein's theory is that this 'social support' is strengthened by a
'restricted code' of communication. Surely, though, this 'social support' is maintained at the cost of alienation from the important
agencies of society. The key factor in this alienation is the passivity
which arises out of an inability to question, to criticize, to communicate. One can argue, on the one hand, that higher education, especially at university level, should be more closely integrated
into the lives of ordinary working people. Whether this happens or
not, however, surely education *must* transcend the purely local
setting. In a simple society, education can be accomplished by
adults explaining to the young in a context the skills and techniques
possessed by all members of that society. But the body of knowledge
available in our culture vastly exceeds the amount that any one
individual can know. Education cannot be seen simply as a vehicle
for the transmission of a few vocational skills. One of its aims
must be to make comprehensible to everyone the working of
society—to make it possible to consider rationally questions which
basically affect us. We cannot as a rule hope to understand both
low temperature physics and economic theory. But we must be
able to ask basic questions about, for example, the uses to which
the findings of specialized research are put, or whether we should
spend more money on training teachers or lecturers. We should all
be able to appreciate that a statement like 'Some coloured immigrants live off National Assistance because they are lazy' is not
logically related to the statement, 'All people who are coloured
should be sent off to their countries of origin'. None of these questions or appraisals can possibly be made if we have never used
the appropriate level of discourse—if, in fact, we can barely manage
to answer simple questions about tennis balls. At a simpler level,
greater participation and power, both in work and in politics, cannot
be available to anyone whose communication skills do not match
up to those presently controlling the official channels. As long as

many people remain in this position, changes in class structure and distribution of power will not happen. We are not suggesting that everyone should struggle to gain a First in English at Cambridge or to enter a fight for white-collar jobs. We suggest that these differences in status and occupation might become less crucial if some sense of power over our bureaucratic agencies could be made more available to everyone.

Theory and practice in education probably get on quite well together. Theories in psychology and sociology, relevant to education, often do not translate easily into specific recommendations. One important exception in psychology has been the derivation of New Maths influenced very much by the work of Jean Piaget. Bernstein's theory, partly sociological, partly psychological, made an immediate impact on educationalists. Like other important theories, it gained its power from relating in one conceptual scheme a number of quite disparate facts and ideas: the theories of linguistic relativity, Durkheim's theories of social integration, the under-achievement of the lower working class in a context of equality of opportunity, the work on the role of language and speech in conceptualization. A theory can be powerful without pointing to any immediate practical applications; this one clearly did.

The programme we have presented is one possible way of developing language skills in children who need them. There are probably other ways. We hope that teachers and students of education who have been excited by Bernstein's work will read, criticize, improve upon and try out the suggestions made in this book.

Postscript

Basil Bernstein

I first started to work on the theory which guided the Gahagans' exploratory language programme in 1956 and since that time it has undergone continuous extension and modification. Theory both guides research and in turn is modified by the research. I shall give here the development as it relates to the central concept of code. The codes were originally defined in terms of social constraints upon syntactic choices realized in the *use* of speech. Now the major difficulty of such a general definition is that it does not take into account the effect of specific contexts upon linguistic choices. Despite the context-free definition of codes, a major focus of our research has been to enquire into both the orientations of mothers towards the use of language in various contexts and the speech of mothers and children evoked by different situations in the context of an interview. As a direct result of this research the concept of code has been developed with specific reference to critical socializing contexts. It is a matter of considerable interest that this later formulation confirms the contextual approach used by the Gahagans in their programme. It may be helpful to the reader to spell out a little more fully *that part of the central concept 'code', which has a bearing upon the major theme of this book.*

First of all, the concept 'code' has nothing to do with such curious terms as standard and sub-standard English. It is not concerned with the *availability* to a child of syntax or even lexes. When we examined the vocabulary of middle-class and working-class five-year-old children, it was intuitively clear that there was not one word offered by the middle-class children which was not available (i.e. in the passive vocabulary) to the working-class children. The differences lay not in availability, but in *use*. The working-class children in the context we created offered a less differentiated vocabulary. In the same way, we found that middle-class children when invited to talk about a descriptive context used, relatively more than working-class children, linguistic expressions of uncertainty

115

(e.g. might be, could be, I wonder, etc.). This does not mean that these expressions are not *available* to working-class children. Of course they are; the point is that the descriptive context we offered evoked these expressions much *less*. Again, working-class children have *access* to syntactic markers of the hypotheticals, disjunctives, conditionals, etc. Every little child in a control context has at some point heard:

'If you do that then . . .'
'Either you . . . or . . .'
'You can do that but . . .'
'Because I tell you.'

However, if we take the instructional contexts, where the mother is exploring the objective nature of persons and things and where the child acquires a variety of skills, we are likely to find that these contexts are numerically greater, cover a greater range of referents, in one social class group than another. Further, that there is a greater use of syntactic markers which make explicit the logical distribution of meaning. Thus the concept restricted code does not specify that linguistic expressions of uncertainty, syntactic markers of the logical distribution of meaning, will never be used or are not available, only that (and 'only' is critical) there is a restriction on the contexts in which they are used.

Let me take this a little further. Following Michael Halliday, Professor of Linguistics, University College London, we can distinguish four critical contexts in the socialization of the child.

1. The regulative context—these are authority relationships where the child is made aware of the rules of the moral order and their various backings.

2. The instructional context, where the child learns about the objective nature of objects and persons, and acquires skills of various kinds.

3. The imaginative or innovating contexts, where the child is encouraged to experiment and re-create his world on his own terms, and in his own way.

4. The interpersonal context, where the child is made aware of affective states—his own, and others.

Now if these four contexts are realized through forms of speech where meanings are implicit, principles infrequently elaborated, qualified or explored, infrequently related to the *specific* experience of the child or the *specific* requirements of the local context, where alternative possibilities are infrequently offered, where questioning is less encouraged, then I have suggested that the *underlying structure* of the communication is regulated through a restricted code. I have also suggested that the linguistic realization of these four socializing contexts will be differently patterned according to the underlying code. Where the code is elaborated, then the speech of the parents in these four contexts of child socialization, will show signs of complex editing; that is, syntax and lexes will be carefully selected in order to make explicit and to qualify the meaning. This does not mean that all contexts will evoke *linguistically* elaborated speech. For example, simplicity may be required in certain instructional contexts. Where the code is elaborated it is likely that the resources of the grammar will be utilized more fully in the shaping of the speech. In this sense, code elaboration entails greater selection and combination from the *same* linguistic resources than does code restriction. Because the code is restricted it does not mean that linguistically elaborated speech variants never occur; because the code is elaborated it does not mean that linguistically restricted speech variants never occur.

We can begin to see that if there is a discrepancy in the meanings and their linguistic realization in the regulative, instructional, imaginative, inter-personal contexts, between the home and the school, then for such children there will be initial difficulties. These difficulties will be intensified if the school does not start with the commonsense every-day world of the child, family and community. The Gahagans in their book have focused upon these four contexts and their programme attempted to encourage the children to explore these contexts in a number of different ways.

My own view has always been that code restriction where it exists does not constitute linguistic or cultural deprivation; for there is a delicacy and variety in cultural and imaginative forms. I can understand, however, that from a specific psychological viewpoint code restrictions may be equated with educational deficit. That there is an educational issue I do not deny, but that is why we have schools. The schools' central task as I see it is to offer *all* children the possibility of exploring the boundaries of man's consciousness in such a way that the boundaries are not experienced as a prison, but as a tension between the known and the possible.

I

Appendix 1

TABLE 1 *Number of children in the three groups of schools at the beginning of the Research*

Group	Boys	Girls	Total
E1	38	37	75
C1	30	32	62
C2	31	41	72
Total	99	110	209

TABLE 2 *Number of children left in the three groups of schools at the end of the Research*

Group	Boys	Girls	Total
E1	29	27	56
C1	26	22	48
C2	21	37	58
Total	76	86	162

TABLE 3 *Means and standard deviations of Matrices raw scores for the three groups of schools*

Group	Boys		Girls		Total	
	Mean	S.D.	Mean	S.D.	Mean	S.D.
E1	13·58	3·35	13·19	2·46	13·39	2·93
C1	13·80	2·75	13·47	3·29	13·63	3·02
C2	13·90	4·80	12·78	2·89	13·26	3·84
Total	13·75	3·68	13·12	2·87	13·41	3·29

TABLE 4 *Means and standard deviations of Crichton Vocabulary raw scores for the three groups of schools*

Group	Boys		Girls		Total	
	Mean	S.D.	Mean	S.D.	Mean	S.D.
E1	18·42	5·67	16·54	7·34	17·49	6·57
C1	16·07	5·05	15·84	7·42	15·95	6·34
C2	16·19	5·39	13·29	4·56	14·54	5·10
Total	17·01	5·46	15·13	6·57	16·02	6·12

TABLE 5 *Means and standard deviations of E.P.V.T. standardized scores for the three groups of schools*

Group	Boys		Girls		Total	
	Mean	S.D.	Mean	S.D.	Mean	S.D.
E1	105·89	13·69	103·08	12·99	104·51	13·34
C1	101·00	15·11	99·53	12·47	100·24	13·72
C2	101·84	13·64	95·22	13·38	98·07	13·80
Total	103·14	14·15	99·12	13·30	101·02	13·78

TABLE 6 *Means and standard deviations of test scores obtained by middle-class children*

	N	Matrices		Crichton		E.P.V.T.	
		Mean	S.D.	Mean	S.D.	Mean	S.D.
Boys	78	14·76	3·40	18·19	5·79	110·87	12·35
Girls	70	15·00	3·02	17·95	5·78	109·95	12·94
Total	148	14·87	3·24	18·08	5·77	110·43	12·68

TABLE 7 *Frequency (proportion) of low, medium and high EPT scorers in three groups of sample schools*

	Low 85 or less	Medium 86 – 114	High 115 or more	Total
E1	3 (·06)	40 (·80)	7 (·14)	50 (1·00)
C1 + C2	27 (·33)	50 (·60)	6 (·07)	83 (1·00)
Total Sample	30 (·23)	90 (·68)	13 (·10)	133 (1·00)

Appendix 2   The Language Programme and the English Progress Test: An Evaluation

W. Brandis   Research Officer, Sociological Research Unit

At the end of the third year of the language programme the 'English Progress Test A2',[1] hereinafter referred to as EPT, was administered to all sample children (except those in one control school). This test fits both the orientation of the language programme and the function of a general educational evaluation, in that it is a measure of attainment in curriculum English.

The EPT is intended for children 7 and 8 years old. It consists of 42 questions grouped into 10 sections, each testing a specific language skill. The child has to read the question and write down the answer, so minimal literacy is a necessary condition for obtaining a score. The child's raw score, which is simply the total number of right answers, is converted to an age-standardized score with mean 100 and standard deviation 15.

The orientation of this paper is towards educationally underprivileged minorities, so a general analysis of the EPT will not be carried out here. Taking EPT scores as the criterion, it is proposed to examine the effect of the language programme only on (i) the incidence of 'poor' performance in English children, and (ii) the general performance of West Indian children.

Method of Analysis

The language programme has been evaluated on the basis of a factorial design which seeks to control fortuitous initial differences in verbal I.Q. Such a design greatly simplifies the controlled comparison of test scores across categories within a selected factor. However, it precludes the comparison of 'natural' social groupings,

121

such as schools, if these are ignored in the factorial composition of the design. Moreover, the application of this design to a sample must, by definition, result in a reduction of sample size, and so the evaluation of an experimental programme on special minority groups within the population of interest could quite easily run out of cases.

Whatever the pros and cons of the factorial design in a general evaluative study, it is clearly inappropriate in the examination of the two problems outlined above, for each is concerned with a group whose incidence in the population sampled is low. In consequence, the factorial design has been abandoned, and in both projects the analysis has been carried out on the maximum possible sample.

In technical terms, it is proposed to partition the total variance of y, the standardized EPT score, into the component due to 1 experimental design levels, the component due to k(1) schools within each experimental level, and the residual component e. Since 1 is a fixed factor and k(1) a random factor, the basic analysis of variance model resolves into:

Est. Mean Square l $= \sigma_e^2 + n\sigma_{k(l)}^2 + nk\sigma_l^2$
Est. Mean Squares $k(l) = \sigma_e^2 + n\sigma_{k(l)}^2$
Est. Mean Squares e $= \sigma_e^2$

If there is no evidence against the null hypothesis that $\sigma^2 k(1) = 0$, then the k(1) and e components will be pooled to provide the denominator for a test of the null hypothesis that $\sigma^2 1 = 0$. In other words, as long as differences between schools may be attributed to the sampling process, they will be treated as part of the error term.

This model of analysis is attractively simple, but there is a problem which, if properly considered, will complicate it. It can be plausibly argued that observed differences in EPT scores are simply a special expression of general I.Q. and attainment differences. Differences between groups may not be unique to the EPT, but general over a population of intelligence and attainment tests, any one of which would have produced the same results. In order to assess the uniqueness of EPT differences, it is necessary to compare the EPT scores with some other test of a similar, though more general, character. The data which most nearly satisfy these requirements are scores derived from an administration of the Wechsler Intelligence Scale for Children (WISC)[3] at the beginning of the third school year.

An analysis of EPT differences, taking into account differences in WISC, may be conducted in one of two different ways: Analysis of Covariance, or Analysis of Variance of Repeated Measures.

Some might argue that the Covariance design is appropriate because EPT differences are thereby controlled for WISC differences. It all depends, however, on what we mean by 'control'. A covariance analysis would test the null hypothesis that differences between groups in EPT scores are a *function* of differences in WISC scores. Our null hypothesis is that differences in EPT scores are *parallel* to differences in WISC scores, that both are a function of differences in a general factor which underlies a hypothesized population of intelligence and attainment tests. The appropriate design for this hypothesis is one which allocates equal status to WISC and EPT, and so it must take the form of an analysis of variance of repeated measures.

However, the conventional representation of a repeated measures design requires some modifications. Texts such as Winer[3] assume that the 'repeated measures' factor is fixed. But this is precisely the research hypothesis which we want to test. Accordingly, it will be initially assumed that the repeated measures are random. If between-group differences on the EPT are significantly different from between-group differences on the WISC, i.e. one of the measures-groups' interactions is significant, then the EPT and WISC are not effectively substitutable, and it will be concluded that, for the problem in hand, they have not been drawn from the same population of tests. The Within-individuals part of the repeated measures design will therefore be used to test the hypothesis of interest, and by the same token, to assess whether EPT and WISC are repeated measures on a fixed or a random factor. This in turn will determine whether certain variances should be included in the Between-individuals part of the Repeated Measures model.

The effect of these considerations on the anova model set out at the beginning of this section is its extension to include a component due to j measures. Letting i stand for individuals, and assuming that j is a random factor, the final model becomes:

Between-individuals

EMS $l \quad = \sigma_e^2 + (\sigma_{ji(kl)}^2 + n\sigma_{jk(l)}^2 + nk\sigma_{jl}^2) + j\sigma_{i(kl)}^2 + nj\sigma_{k(l)}^2 + nkj\sigma_i^2$

EMS $k(l) = \sigma_e^2 + (\sigma_{ji(kl)}^2 + n\sigma_{jk(l)}^2) \quad + j\sigma_{i(kl)}^2 + nj\sigma_{k(l)}^2$

EMS $i(kl) = \sigma_e^2 + (\sigma^2_{ji(kl)}) + j\sigma_{i(kl)}^2$

Within-individuals

EMS $j \quad = \sigma_e^2 + \sigma_{ji(kl)}^2 + n\sigma_{jk(l)}^2 + nkl\sigma_j^2$

EMS $jl \quad = \sigma_e^2 + \sigma_{ji(kl)}^2 + n\sigma_{jk(l)}^2 + nk\sigma_{jl}^2$

EMS $jk(l) \ = \sigma_e^2 + \sigma_{ji(kl)}^2 + n\sigma_{jk(l)}^2$

EMS $ji(kl) = \sigma_e^2 + \sigma_{ji(kl)}^2$

The bracketed terms in the Between-individuals part are included in the model only if the assumption that j is random is not disputed by data in the Within-individuals part, or, more formally, if there is insufficient evidence against the null hypothesis that $\sigma^2_{jk(l)} = \sigma^2_{jl} = 0$. Finally, where there is no evidence against the null hypothesis that a population variance is equal to zero, the degrees of freedom and sum of squares associated with that variance will, as before, be combined with those which produce the denominator of the non-significant F-ratio.

RESULTS

1.   The Incidence of Low EPT Scorers

A simple criterion of 'low' scoring on the EPT is one standard deviation below the mean, i.e. 85 or less. For comparison, those scoring 115 and above may be designated 'high' scorers. The distribution of score categories by school within experimental level is shown in table 1.

If differences in the incidence of low scoring were a function of differences through the whole EPT scale, then they would be reflected in a parallel differential incidence of high scorers. Table 1, however, indicates that the incidence of low scoring is distinctly more variable than that of high scoring. To emphasize this point, table 2 shows two analyses of variance, the first taking the proportion of low scorers as the criterion, and the second taking the proportion of high scorers as the criterion.

In neither analysis is there sufficient evidence against the null hypothesis that $\sigma^2_{k(l)} = 0 (p > \cdot 1$ in each case), so the $k(l)$ and $i(kl)$ terms are pooled and designated $i(l)$. This pooled term produces the denominator for the F-ratio which is used to test the null hypothesis that $\sigma^2_l = 0$. There is no hint of a significant difference between experimental levels in the proportion of high scorers, but the difference in the proportion of low scorers is dramatically significant. It is quite evident that the experimental design has been far more effective in disturbing patterns of low EPT scoring than those of high EPT scoring.

The nature of this disturbance is clear from table 1. The three schools with the smallest proportion of low scorers are also the three experimental schools—the direct probability of an event as extreme as this occurring by chance is 1 in 56. On the other hand, the generalized programme of intervention in the C2 schools appears to

TABLE 1 *Frequency/proportion of low, medium, and high EPT scorers in sample schools*

			Low: 85 or less	Mid: 86–114	High: 115 of more	Total
1	Experimental	A	2/·13	12/·80	1/·01	15/1·00
	schools	B	1/·06	14/·82	2/·12	17/1·00
		C	0/·00	14/·78	4/·22	18/1·00
		Total	3/·06	40/·80	7/·14	50/1·00
2	control	D	9/·60	6/·40	0/·00	15/1·00
	schools 2	E	4/·24	10/·59	3/·18	17/1·00
		F	5/·29	10/·59	2/·12	17/1·00
		Total	18/·37	26/·53	5/·10	49/1·00
3	control	G	3/·25	8/·67	1/·08	12/1·00
	schools 1	H		(EPT not administered)*		
		I	6/·27	16/·73	0/·00	22/1·00
		Total	9/·26	24/·71	1/·03	34/1·00
	grand total		30/·23	90/·68	13/·10	133/·100

TABLE 2 *Variance components of two sets of dichotomized (unit interval) EPT scores*

(i) y = Low scoring, Remainder

MS i 23·234|132 =   ·176
MS l 2·408|2   = 1·204; $F_{2,130}$ = 7·52, p < ·001
MS $i(l)$ 20·826|130 =   ·160
MS $k(l)$ 1·348|5   =   ·270; $F_{5,125}$ = 1·73, not sig.
MS $i(kl)$ 19·478|125 =   ·156

(ii) y = High scoring, Remainder

MS i 11·729|132 =   ·089
MS l ·248|2   =   ·124; $F_{2,130}$ = 1·40, not sig.
MS $i(l)$ 11·481|130 =   ·088
MS $k(l)$ ·519|5   =   ·104; $F_{5,125}$ = 1·18, not sig.
MS $i(kl)$ 10·962|125 =   ·088

* Owing to the end-of-term activities it was not possible to give the test to the children of this school.

have done absolutely nothing to reduce the incidence of low EPT scoring. Indeed, with the notable exception of School D, where no less than 60% of the children are low scorers, the control schools 2 and control schools 1 produce a remarkably uniform proportion of low scorers, varying by a maximum of 3% around a mean of 26%[4]. Before considering the role of WISC, these data may be explored a little further by making use of known parameters of the EPT. The test is standardised in such a way that one-sixth of all children in the appropriate age-range should score 85 or less. So the expected proportion of low scorers in a random sample is ·167, and the difference between observed and expected proportions may be tested for significance in any group of schools. Even when the somewhat volatile School D is excluded, the combined C2 and C1 schools contain a significantly higher proportion of low EPT scorers than would be expected on a general random sampling basis ($\chi_1^2 = F_{1,\infty} = Z^2 = 4.70$; $p < ·05$). In other words, the proportion of low scorers is predictably higher in a normal sample of working-class children than in the overall population. However, what is really astonishing is that the experimental schools actually contain a significantly smaller proportion of low EPT scorers than the general population ($\chi_1^2 = F_{1,\infty} = Z^2 = 4.09$; $p < ·05$).

How far are the observed differences in the incidence of low EPT scoring a reflection of parallel differences in low IQ scoring? Since WISC is standardized with precisely the same norms as the EPT, 'low' scoring on the WISC might reasonably be set at scores of 85 and under. Unfortunately, the standardization of the WISC is American, and although the test has been amended for British consumption, it has not been re-standardized in terms of the published mean and standard deviation. In the sample of schools considered here, the mean WISC scores hover around 100, which would, under normal circumstances, be rather unusual for working-class children. We can only assume that the British population mean for the amended test is higher than 100. It is not surprising, then, that only 14 children obtained a WISC IQ of 85 or less. Even taking 90 and less as 'low' scoring on the WISC produces only 24 children, as against 30 children at 85 and less on the EPT. However, this is the cut-off point which will be taken, so 'low' WISC is set at scores of 90 and under.

The distribution of low EPT scoring is compared with that of low WISC scoring in table 3. and the analysis of variance associated with these data is set out in table 4.

The chain of reasoning by which the F-ratios in table 4 were produced should not present much difficulty. There is absolutely no evidence

TABLE 3 *Frequency/proportion of low EPT and low WISC scorers in sample schools*

			Low EPT: 85 or less	Low WISC: 90 or less	Difference in proportions	n
1	experimental	A	2/·13	2/·13	·00	15
	schools	B	1/·06	1/·06	·00	17
		C	0/·00	2/·11	−·11	18
		Total	3/·06	5/·10	−·04	50
2	control	D	9/·60	3/·20	+·40	15
	schools 2	E	4/·24	2/·12	+·12	17
		F	5/·29	1/·06	+·24	17
		Total	18/·37	6/·12	+·24	49
3	control	G	3/·25	4/·33	−·08	12
	schools 1	I	6/·27	9/·41	−·14	22
		Total	9/·26	13/·38	−·12	34
	grand total		30/·23	24/·18	+·05	133

TABLE 4 *Variance components of joint WISC and EPT scores, each dichotomised on a unit interval scale into low scores against Remainder*

Between-individuals

MS l $= 2 \cdot 673 | 2 = 1 \cdot 336$ $F_{2,130} = 6 \cdot 13\ p < \cdot 01,\ \sigma_l^2 \neq 0$
MS $i(l)$ $= 28 \cdot 366 | 130 = \cdot 218$
MS $k(l)$ $= 1 \cdot 198 | 5 = \cdot 240$ $F_{5,125} = 1 \cdot 10,$ not sig., $\sigma_{k(l)}^2 = 0$
MS $i(kl)$ $= 27 \cdot 168 | 125 = \cdot 217$

Within-individuals

MS j (arbitrary)
MS jl $= 1 \cdot 609 | 2 = \cdot 804$ $F_{2,130} = 10 \cdot 20,\ p < \cdot 001,\ \sigma_{jl}^2 \neq 0,$
                                              & factor j is fixed
MS $ji(l)$ $= 10 \cdot 256 | 130 = \cdot 079$
MS $jk(l)$ $= \cdot 402 | 5 = \cdot 081$ $F_{5,125} = 1 \cdot 02,$ not sig., $\sigma_{jk(l)}^2 = 0$
MS $ji(kl)$ $= 9 \cdot 854 | 125 = \cdot 079$

against the null hypothesis that $\sigma^2_{jk(l)} = 0$, so the $ji(kl)$ and $jk(l)$ terms are pooled and designated $ji(l)$. The null hypothesis that $\sigma^2_{ji} = 0$ is, however, conclusively rejected, so the repeated measures factor must be considered fixed. Accordingly, tests of significance in the between-individuals section are completely autonomous of the within-individuals data. Again, there is no evidence against the null hypothesis that $\sigma^2_{k(l)} = 0$, so the $k(l)$ and $i(kl)$ terms are pooled and designated $i(l)$. Finally, the null hypothesis that $\sigma^2_i = 0$ is once more rejected. The analysis clearly indicates that all variation between schools within experimental levels may be attributed to the sampling process, whereas all variation between experimental levels is significantly greater than would be expected on a random sampling basis. The fundamentally important finding, of course, is that $\sigma^2_{ji} \neq 0$, thus showing that differences between experimental levels in the incidence of low EPT scoring are, within this simple repeated measures design, unique to the EPT. Table 3 indicates quite clearly that their uniqueness is due to the performance of the C2 schools. In each one of these three schools, the incidence of low EPT scoring is much greater than that of low WISC scoring; in every other school it is either the same or it is less. The reason for this is also evident from table 3. The incidence of low EPT scoring in the C2 schools is as high as in the control schools, but in the same group the incidence of low WISC scoring is as low as in the experimental schools. Table 5 shows the consequences of this process in particularly dramatic form.

The mean WISC scores of low EPT scorers in the experimental and control schools are suitably low at between 80 and 85, but the mean WISC scores of the C2 schools vary from 95 to as high as 105.

Before drawing conclusions about the effect of the experimental design on the joint distribution of low EPT and low WISC scores, it is necessary to consider initial pre-experimental differences in low scoring on some related test, preferably of IQ. Only one standardized set of pretest scores is available, and these have been obtained from the English Version of the Peabody Picture Vocabulary Test (EPVT). Setting 'low' scoring at 90 and under (for very much the same reasons as with the WISC) gives the distribution shown in table 6.

Although the experimental schools began with a slightly lower proportion of low IQ children, the same certainly cannot be said of the C2 schools. In fact, it turns out that there is insufficient evidence against the null hypotheses that $\sigma^2_{k(l)} = 0$ and $\sigma^2_i = 0$ ($p > \cdot 1$ in both cases). The observed variation in the incidence of low EPVT scoring may therefore be attributed to the sampling process. Not surprisingly, an analysis of covariance on the data in table 3, treating EPVT as the covariate, has virtually no effect on the anova

TABLE 5   *Mean WISC scores of low EPT scorers*

			n	Mean WISC
1	experimental	A	2	85·0
	schools	B	1	80·0
		C	0	–
		total	3	83·3
2	control	D	9	95·9
	schools 2	E	4	100·0
		F	5	104·6
		total	18	99·3
3	control	G	3	83·3
	schools 1	I	6	83·3
		total	9	83·3

TABLE 6   *Frequency/proportion of low EPVT 'pretest' scores in the terminal sample*

			Low EPVT: 90 or less	Remainder: 91 or more	Total
1	experimental	A	3/·20	12/·80	15/1·00
	schools	B	2/·12	15/·88	17/1·00
		C	4/·22	14/·78	18/1·00
			9/·18	41/·82	50/1·00
2	control	D	2/·13	13/·81	15/1·00
	schools 2	E	4/·24	13/·76	17/1·00
		F	7/·41	10/·59	17/1·00
			13/·27	36/·73	49/1·00
3	control	G	3/·25	9/·75	12/1·00
	schools 1	I	4/·18	18/·82	22/1·00
			7/·21	27/·79	34/1·00
	grand total		29/·22	104/·78	133/1·00

results set out in table 4. Therefore significant between-group variation in the joint distribution of WISC and EPT low scoring appears to be a consequence entirely of the experimental design.

It might be argued that the allocation of EPT and WISC scores to arbitrary categories of 'low' and 'not-low' could have capitalized on differences which are peculiarly local to the cut-off points used for the two sets of scores. This potential objection can be countered by using the full range of scores to calculate EPT and WISC means (table 7), and to repeat the critical within-individuals analysis of variance (table 8).

It is evident that the distribution of mean scores in table 7 faithfully reflects the pattern of low scoring indicated in table 3, and this is

TABLE 7 *Mean EPT & WISC scores in sample schools*

			Mean EPT	Mean WISC	Mean (EPT-WISC)	12
1	experimental	A	100·3	112·1	−11·8	15
	schools	B	101·0	110·2	− 9·2	17
		C	104·9	106·3	− 1·4	18
		total	102·2	109·3	− 7·1	50
2	control	D	81·6	97·0	−15·4	15
	schools 2	E	97·8	112·2	−14·4	17
		F	97·5	116·4	−18·9	17
		total	92·7	109·0	−16·3	49
3	control	G	99·8	102·5	− 2·6	12
	schools 1	I	92·5	95·5	− 3·0	22
		total	95·1	97·9	− 2·8	34
	grand total		96·9	105·5	− 8·6	133

TABLE 8 *Within-individuals variance components of joint WISC and EPT scores*

MS jl 1,993·226/2   = 996·613 $F_{2,130} = 14·30$, $p < ·001 \sigma_{jl}^2 \neq 0$
MS $ji(l)$ 9,058·985/130 = 69·684
MS $jk(l)$ 448·631/5   = 89·726 $F_{5,125} = 1·30$, not sig, $\sigma jk(l)^2 = 0$
MS $ji(kl)$ 8,610·355/125 = 68·883

confirmed by the emphatic rejection, once more, of the null hypothesis that $\sigma_{ji}^2 = 0$.

So, the higher EPT mean score, like the reduced incidence of 'low' EPT scoring, appears to be uniquely associated with the experimental language programme.

Before concluding this section, attention must be drawn to one further problem. The published probability levels for F-ratios assume normality of the sampling distribution, so departures from normality alter the probability of obtaining a given F-ratio. The sampling distribution is a function of the population distribution, approaching normality as sample size becomes large. Now the population distribution in this study is, by definition, highly skewed, for the EPT has been set so that only 17 % of the population at large should score 85 and under.

However, the eight schools under consideration produce a sample size of 133, which many authorities would consider quite large enough to cover at least moderate departures from normality in the population sampled. Moreover, the sample is drawn from a working-class population, which, on the evidence of the C2 and C1 schools, have a higher proportion of low EPT scorers and therefore a less skewed distribution in terms of the primary criterion. It is likely, then, that reliance on the probability of achieving the calculated F-ratios need not be questioned too severely. Finally, the F-ratios produced by the variation between experimental groups are so large that a moderate shift from the published probability levels must still leave results that are significant.

So the conclusion suggested by the analysis set out in table 4 seems inescapable. Within the population sampled, any programme designed to aid the educationally underprivileged, and administered with sufficient vigour, will reduce the incidence of low IQ scoring (represented here by the WISC); but it specifically needs a language programme to reduce the incidence of low Engish Attainment scoring (represented here by the EPT). The language programme, then, has reduced low scoring on the EPT, and it must have done so by pulling up children who would otherwise have obtained low EPT scores. And that is, after all, what was supposed to happen. The programme was quite specifically oriented to those who, educationally, would suffer most from the discontinuity between the communication style of the family system and that of the educational system. It is for this reason that working-class schools were originally chosen for the programme. The results indicate that the primary objective of the language programme has, to a large extent, been achieved.

2.   Children of West Indian Origin

Up to this point, evaluation of the language programme has always excluded children of West Indian origin. Although the programme was not specifically intended for these children, they are likely to be even more dramatically underprivileged in educational terms than those for whom it was intended. So it is of considerable interest to assess whether West Indian children have been affected by the language programme.

There are 11 West Indian children in the sample, 5 in a school from the C2 group, and the other 6 equally divided between two experimental schools (B and C). Taking standardized EPT and WISC scores as the repeated measures criterion, and standardized EPVT scores as the pretest covariate, this small sample will, as far as possible, be subjected to the kind of formal analysis conducted in the previous section. However, because the West Indian sample covers only 3 schools within 2 experimental levels, estimates of between-group variance are necessarily more restricted. The l and jl terms refer now to a simple comparison between experimental and C2 children. The restriction on $k(l)$ and $jk(l)$ is rather more serious, for these are now based on the difference between schools B and C alone. In testing null hypotheses associated with the K terms, the F-ratio denominator, as well as its numerator, will be limited to data from the experimental schools.

Table 7 shows the distribution and mean test scores of the WestIndian sample by school, and table 8 shows a simple analysis of variance with EPT as the criterion.

The observed differences in mean EPT must evidently be ascribed to chance, but once again, it is possible to capitalize on the published parameters of the EPT, namely that $\mu = 100$ and $\sigma = 15$ .Taking the population standard deviation to estimate the variance of the sampling distribution, it is possible to show how far the difference between observed means and the population mean may be attributed to the sampling process. In one group only is this difference significant. School E produces a significantly lower mean EPT score than would be expected on a random sampling basis ($\chi_l^2 = F_{l, \infty} = Z^2 = 5.69$; $p < \cdot 05$), and, of course, this is the one school that did not have the language programme. But as the experimental schools do not differ significantly either from the general population or from School E, this result must be considered inconclusive.

Table 11 shows what happens when the EPT scores are analysed in conjunction with the WISC scores.

The null hypothesis that $\sigma_{jl}^2 = 0$ is clearly rejected. This means that

TABLE 9 *Distribution of the West Indian sample by school, with mean EPVT, WISC, and EPT scores*

experimental	n	Mean EPVT	Mean WISC	Mean EPT
school B	3	82·3	88·7	88·7
school C	3	88·3	97·7	104·0
total experimental	6	85·3	93·2	96·3
school E (C.2)	5	86·4	90·4	84·0
grand total	11	85·8	91·9	90·7

TABLE 10 *Variance components of standardized EPT scores in the West Indian sample*

MS l =   414·8|1 = 414·8 $F_{1,9}$ = 1·03, not sig. $\sigma_l^2 = 0$
MS $i(l)$ = 3,609·3|9 = 401·0
MS k =   352·7|1 = 352·7 $F_{1,4}$ < 1·00, not sig. $\sigma_k^2 = 0$
MS $i(k)$ = 1,492·7|4 = 373·2

TABLE 11 *Variance components of joint WISC and EPT scores in the West Indian sample*

Between-individuals

MS l =   310·923|1 = 310·923 $F_{1,9}$ < 1·00, not sig. $\sigma_l^2 = 0$
MS $i(l)$ = 6,524·350|9 = 724·928
MS k^* =   444 ·083|1 = 444·083 $F_{1,4}$ < 1·00, not sig. $\sigma_k^2 = 0$
MS $i(k)^*$ = 3,182·667|4 = 795·667

Within-individuals

MS jl = 124·802|1 = 124·802 $F_{1,9}$ = 8·20, $p < ·05$ $\sigma_{jl}^2 \neq 0$
MS $ji(l)$ = 137·017|9 = 15·224
MS jk^* = 30·083|1 = 30·083 $F_{1,4}$ = 1·96, not sig. $\sigma_{jk}^2 = 0$
MS $ji(k)^*$ = 61·333|4 = 15·333

* Experimental Schools only.

K

the difference between the experimental schools and the C2 School E in mean EPT scores is significantly different from the comparable difference in mean WISC scores. In effect, the high correlation between WISC and EPT has transformed an apparently chance difference into a difference that is respectably significant. And it is certainly in the predicted direction. A comparison between tables 3 and 7 reveals that the mean WISC and EPT scores in the experimental and C2 schools follows much the same pattern for West Indian children as for English children. Given the nature of the sample, how far can we infer that the difference between experimental and C2 West Indians in controlled EPT scores is due to the language programme?

Curiously enough, the case against making such an inference does not rest on the smallness of the sample size, for this is properly accommodated within the framework of the analysis. The problem is the reduced number of schools, and particularly that only one school outside the language programme is represented in the sample. In effect, the analysis has assumed that $\sigma^2k(1) = 0$, the only evidence for this being that schools B and C are not significantly different. However, table 3 does show that School E is nicely representative when judged in terms of the low WISC and EPT scoring patterns discussed in the previous section. Moreover, table 7 shows that the West Indian children in C2 School E have much the same mean IQ as their peers in the experimental schools, not only on the post-test WISC, but on the pre-test EPVT. Indeed, using analysis of covariance to control EPT and WISC scores for the initial EPVT scores has virtually no effect whatever on the results reported in table 9. So it is unlikely that the West Indian children in C2 School E differed in any critical way from their experimental peers when they first went to school—for example, because of selective parental migration to different catchment areas.

It therefore seems reasonable to conclude that the language programme has been effective in raising the mean EPT scores of West Indian children, as well as in reducing the incidence of low scoring among English children. This result is remarkable for two quite separate reasons: (i) because small samples need large differences in order to produce statistically significant results; and (ii) because the language programme was not in any way oriented to the unique linguistic problems of West Indian children. In view of the findings, some comment on the nature of those linguistic problems is in order.

West Indian children are not expected to perform as well as English children on tests designed for English children. If school children in England had to perform on IQ tests designed for West

Indians, it would no doubt be found that the indigenous English child is remarkably stupid, fit only for a non-academic school career, and, at best, the job of bus-conductor thereafter. This interesting conclusion would be a consequence of the unavoidable culture-specificity of all tests, even IQ tests. A quick perusal of the WISC, for example, will reveal that it is brimming with culture-specific symbols. So when West Indian children score an average of 86 on the EPVT and 92 on the WISC, it is perhaps more appropriate to question the relevance of the tests as instruments of comparison than to make nasty comments about the IQ of the testees.

There is, then, an expected test-performance gap between different cultural groups which may be entirely attributed to the culture-specificity of a test's symbolic content. Now the language programme was oriented specifically to the linguistic problems of the English working-class child, as defined by the standards of the educational system. It has, by intention, been successful in (temporarily) reducing the casualty figures of English working-class children in the educational system, but it has done the same for West Indian children, and this was not explicitly intended. So the linguistic problems of West Indian children in the English educational system have, in part, fallen within the orbit of a programme designed only for English working-class children. It would be intriguing to know how far a similarly effective language programme designed specifically for West Indians would differ from the programme used in this research. Such knowledge would indicate the extent and character of the linguistic problems that are common to both groups, and, in particular, the degree to which the common element is simply a matter of symbolic representation, or is interwoven with the more fundamental linguistic processes suggested by Bernstein.

Conclusion

The EPT is designed to test a child's ability to manipulate the written word. Scores derived from its administration are used to measure educational attainment in general literacy, a vital component of the primary school curriculum. Given the usual reservations of test theory, a low EPT score means, quite simply, a low level of one kind of educational attainment. The use of EPT scores to evaluate the language intervention programme is therefore an assessment of that programme's relevance to the educational system.

It is planned to study the EPT scores more fully within a comprehensive programme of analysis which will incorporate Reading Ability scores, three (annual) waves of Verbal and Performance

IQ scores, sex, social class, and the mothers' orientation towards communication and control, all within the framework of the anova models set out in the beginning of this paper. The two studies reported above can in no sense be regarded as a full analysis of the EPT scores. Each has a specific objective, and neither has attempted to explore the results obtained beyond its defined objective.

But within their limits, the two studies do give a clear indication of the effect of the language programme. The use of EPT scores as a criterion emphasizes that the programme has been effective within the Educational System's own terms of reference. It has helped those children who, by the System's standards, would have been the most seriously handicapped, and, above all, it has done so by improving their ability to handle the English language of the Educational System, which is precisely what was intended.

Notes

[1] Published by the National Foundation for Educational Research in England and Wales.
[2] Wechsler, D. 'WISC Manual' (1949); Scottish Council for Research in Education 'Manual for Scottish Standardization of the WISC' (1965).
[3] Winer, B. J. 'Statistical Principles in Experimental Design' (1962).
[4] School D is the only school from the experimental design in which the children had two successive teachers during an academic year. No doubt the remarkably high rate of low EPT scoring in School D could, in part, be attributed to this instability of the second-year teaching arrangements. It should be added that the variation in low scoring between the remaining four non-experimental schools is so slight that it actually achieves significant homogeneity ($x_3^2 = 0.15, p < .02$). The educational problems posed by a working-class intake seems to induce a high English language failure-rate of great consistency in the modal classroom system.

Appendix 3 Differences in the Control of Others

J. Cook, W. Brandis, and M. Goldberg

When the mothers of the sample children were interviewed six months before their children first went to school, they were asked six hypothetical questions about how they would control their child. Two and a half years later, at the end of the children's second year at school, the six questions with appropriate modifications were put to the child. This provided us with a unique opportunity to examine whether the language programme had possibly affected the control styles of the children in the E1 schools. If there were no differences between the E1 and the non-E1 schools on the following:

(1) social class position of the parents,

(2) the mothers' styles,

(3) the mean I.Q. of the children in the two groups of schools, then we would be in a strong position to infer that if the E1 children's control styles were different from the non-E1, this difference could be attributed in some way to the effect of the language programme on the teacher, or children, or both. *We found that there were no differences between the control styles of the mothers, or their social class position, or the I.Q. of the children.*

We now give the six questions which were put to the mother, and the six questions which were put to the child.

To the mother

'Here are some every-day problems which mothers have told us come up with children.'

137

1. 'Supposing you thought it was time —— went to bed, but he started to cry because he wanted to watch something on T.V. What would you say or do?'

2. 'What would you say or do if —— wasn't watching what he was doing and spilt tea over the tablecloth? What would you say or do if he took no notice?'

3. 'What would you do if —— brought you a bunch of flowers, and you found out he had got them from a neighbour's garden?'

4. 'Supposing your husband forgot to bring —— a present that he'd promised, and he wouldn't talk to his father all day. What would you say or do?'
   Probe: 'Supposing —— still wouldn't talk to his father?'

5. 'Imagine —— has started school, and one day he says, "I don't want to go to school today" but he's not ill or anything, but just doesn't want to go. What would you say or do?'
   Probe: 'If after that —— began crying and saying "I don't want to go"?'

6. 'Imagine —— has been out shopping with you, and when you got home you found he'd picked up some little thing from one of the counters without you noticing. What would you say or do?'

To the child

'We're going to talk about some things that can happen at home.'

1. 'Mummy says it's time to go to bed, and the little boy cries because he wants to watch something on T.V.' (brief pause) 'What does Mummy do about that?' (If no mother's speech is given, ask 'What does Mummy say?') 'What will the little boy do then?'

2. 'The little boy isn't looking what he is doing. He spills the tea over the tablecloth.' (brief pause) 'What does Mummy do about that?' (If no mother's speech is given, ask 'What does Mummy say?') 'What will the little boy do then?'

3. 'The little boy's father has forgotten to bring a present that he'd promised him, so the little boy won't talk to him.' (brief pause) 'What does Mummy do about that?' (If no mother's speech is given, ask 'What does Mummy say?') 'What will the little boy do then?'

4. 'Now it's breakfast time. The little boy has said, "I don't want to go to school today", but he is not ill or anything. He does not

want to go.' (brief pause) 'What does Mummy do about that?'
(If no mother's speech is given, ask 'What does Mummy say?')
'What will the little boy do then?'

5. 'The little boy and his Mummy have been shopping. When they
get home Mummy finds out that the little boy has picked up
something in the shop and brought it home without paying for it.'
(brief pause). 'What does Mummy do about that?' (If no mother's
speech is given, ask 'What does Mummy say?') 'What will the
little boy do then?'

6. 'The little boy has brought his mother a bunch of flowers, but he
has taken them from the garden of the lady next door.' (brief
pause). 'What does Mummy do about that?' (If no mother's
speech is given, ask 'What does Mummy say?') 'What will the
little boy do then?'

Sample

The children are drawn from a sample which has been the subject
of a detailed analysis of maternal and child patterns of control
carried out by Jenny Cook, Research Officer, Sociological Research
Unit. In order to carry out this analysis, Miss Cook had to select
children for whom we had a complete set of ability scores and
speech samples, and whose mothers had received the full interview
schedule before the children went to school. Now, as the Gahagans
have explained earlier in this monograph, the parents of the children
in control group schools did not receive the full interview. We
collected only background information from this group of mothers
as we did not want to disturb the function of this control group
as a basic control group. Consequently, the sample used for this
analysis does *not* contain any mothers or any children from the
three schools which make up control group. The final sample thus
consists of:

(*a*) 42 children from the three E1 schools,
(*b*) 42 children from the three control group 2 schools.

The control styles

Miss Jenny Cook has developed an analysis of maternal and child
control styles. This will be written up in detail in a future Sociological Research Unit Monograph. Here we give only a brief description of three styles of the total five we chose for our comparisons.

We carried out the analysis on only three styles because the children offered far too few responses on two of the styles. We now give the three styles:

(1) Punishing

The punishing style is characterized by responses such as:
'Mummy will smack him';
'She'd tell him he was a naughty boy and put him to bed';
'She'd switch the television off and carry him upstairs';
'Mummy would be very angry with him.'

(2) Firmness

This style is characterized by the following responses:
'Mummy would tell him to be careful and watch what he was doing';
'Mummy would wipe it up (the spilt tea) and say be careful next time';
'Mummy would say, "You must go to bed, it's your bed time".'

(3) Mediating

This style is more complex than the above styles and covers a wide range of behaviours:
'Mum would let him stay up. She'd say, "All right, you can watch just for five minutes more".'
'Mum will say, "If you watch the programme tonight you can't see it tomorrow".'
'Mummy would ask the little boy why he didn't want to go to school. She'd tell him that he'd miss his friends if he didn't go.'
'Mum would say, "Never mind, you didn't mean it".'
'Mum would make the little boy take them (the flowers) back. She'd tell him to say sorry to the lady next door.'
'Dad would say, "I forgot your present, I'll get it for you to-morrow".'
This style is called mediating, for it indicates that the child is not relying solely upon an assertion of power or authority but can use more flexible forms of control which involve concession, some understanding of the point of view of the controller *and* of the controlled, and some idea of the consequences of the act for the child *or* some other person.

We are interested only in the number of children who offered mediating styles. This was because this style is linguistically more elaborated; it involves some manipulation of the authority relationship away from a coercive relation, and it indicates that the child has access to a range of alternatives in the context of control. We therefore expected that the E1 children would offer more mediating responses than the non-E1 children.

Table 1 shows the distribution of mediating responses by school of respondent, and Table 2 the analysis of variance which was carried out on the data in Table 1.

T A B L E 1 *Frequency of Mediating Response Styles in E1 and C2 schools*

Number of Mediation Responses

School	0	1	2	3	4	5	6	No. of Children	Mean Score
11	1	3	5	3	2	2		16	2·50
12	3	4	2	4	1			14	1·71
13	1	2	4	3	1	1		12	2·33
Group E1	5	9	11	10	4	3		42	2·19
21	1	7	5	3	1			17	1·76
22	3	3	3		2			11	1·55
23	2	7	2	2	1			14	1·50
Group C2	6	17	10	5	4			42	1·62
Total	11	26	21	15	8	3		84	1·90

T A B L E 2 *Analysis of Variance on the data in Table 1, showing Sums of Squares (SS), degrees of freedom (df), Mean Squares (MS), and F-ratios*

	SS	df	MS	F-ratio
Total	143·239	83		
Between Groups	6·858	1	6·858	$F_{1,82} = 4·12, p < ·05$
Within Groups	136·381	82	1·663	
E1: Total	80·476	41		
Between Schools	4·952	2	2·476	$F_{2,39} = 1·28$, not significant
Within Schools	75·524	39	1·937	
C2: Total	55·905	41		
Between Schools	·619	2	·310	$F_{2,39} = 1·00$, not significant
Within Schools	55·286	39	1·417	

The results in Table 2 clearly indicate that both the E1 and the C2 groups are internally consistent in terms of the school means, and so no school contributes excessively to its respective group mean. However, the difference between E1 and C2 children has produced an F-ratio which is just significant at the ·05 level. Accordingly, the difference between the two groups, each internally homogeneous, cannot be attributed to the sampling process, and the explanation for that difference must be sought in the different programmes which their respective children have undergone.

It is clear, then, that there is a move on the part of the E1 children towards mediating control styles. The children were not *deliberately* trained to make those responses. On the other hand, some of the picture story series did raise questions of adults controlling children, and children controlling other children. The only other influence upon the control styles of the children was the control style of the teachers. Each group of children in each school would have had two teachers, one for the first year, and one for the second year. If the control style of the teacher was affecting the children, then why was there no difference between the children in the three non-E1 schools? If the language programme had affected the control styles of the six teachers of the E1 children, and these styles had indeed affected the children, then we would have had an even more exciting result. A programme which ran for only twenty minutes a day produced changes in the control styles of the teachers! We think that this is somewhat unlikely, and the trend in the E1 children's control styles is much more likely to be the result of the language programme.

We can think of only one other reason for the difference between E1 and non-E1 children. If all the six E1 teachers initially (that is, before they worked on the programme) had similar control styles, but different control styles from the control styles of the six C2 teachers, we might expect the trend we found. However, since the direct probability of this occurrence is 1 in 924, we would suggest that it is a most unlikely explanation.

We therefore conclude that not only has there been an improvement in the E1 children's ability to deal with certain linguistic and cognitive tasks relative to non-E1 children, but also that the E1 children's control styles, as revealed in the situation we constructed, involve less coercive and more linguistically elaborated, more flexible approaches to the control of others.

We should emphasize again that there was no significant difference in the control style of mothers of the children in these two groups of schools, no significant difference in the social class position of the mothers, and no significant difference in the ability scores of the children. The difference between the E1 and C2 children is significant only at the ·05 level. This result should be regarded as no more than highly suggestive. Our view is that the area we have opened up warrants further research into the relationships between speech forms and social control.

References

Abbreviations:

Brit. J. Sociol. *British Journal of Sociology (London)*
J. Child Psychol. & Psychiat. *Journal of Child Psychology and Psychiatry (London)*
Child Developm. *Child Development (Chicago)*

1 Quoted in Secord, P. F. & Backman, C. W., *Social Psychology* (New York: McGraw-Hill, 1964), p. 52.

2 Douglas, J. W. B., *The Home and the School*: a study of ability and attainment in the primary schools (London: MacGibbon & Kee, 1964).

3 Bernstein, B., 'Some sociological determinants of perception: an enquiry into sub-cultural differences', *Brit. J. Sociol.*, Vol. 9, (1958), p. 159. Bernstein, B., 'A public language: some sociological implications of a linguistic form'. *Brit. J. Sociol.*, Vol. 10, (1959), p. 311. Bernstein, B., 'Language and social class', *Brit. J. Sociol.*, Vol. 11, (1960), p. 217. Bernstein, B., 'Aspects of language and learning in the genesis of the social process', *J. Child Psychol. & Psychiat.*, Vol. 1, (1961), p. 313. Bernstein B., 'Social class and linguistic development: a theory of social learning', in *Education, Economy and Society*, eds. Halsey, A. H., Floud, J., & Anderson, C. A. (New York: Free Press, 1961), p. 288. Bernstein, B., 'Linguistic codes, hesitation phenomena and intelligence', *Language & Speech*, Vol. 5, (1962), p. 31. Bernstein, B., 'Social class, linguistic codes and grammatical elements', *Language & Speech*, Vol. 5, (1962), p. 221. Bernstein, B., 'Elaborated and restricted codes: their social origins and some consequences', in *The Ethnography of Communication*, eds. Gumperz, J. & Hymes, D., American Anthropologist Special Publication, 66, No. 6, Part 2, 1964. [Reprinted in *Communication and Culture*, ed. Smith, A. G. (New York: Holt, Rinehart & Winston, 1966).]
Bernstein, B., 'A socio-linguistic approach to social learning', in *Social Science Survey*, ed. Gould, J. (London: Penguin, 1965). Bernstein, B., 'A socio-linguistic approach to socialization: with some reference to educability', in *Directions in Sociolinguistics*, eds. Gumperz, J. & Hymes, D. (New York: Holt, Rinehart & Winston, in press). Also in *Human Context*, Vol. 1, (1968).

4 Bernstein, B., 'Social class, linguistic codes and grammatical elements', *Language & Speech*, Vol. 5, (1962), p. 221.

5 Turner, G. T. & Mohan, B. A., *A Linguistic Description and Computer Program for Children's Speech. (Primary Socialisation, Language and Education, Vol. II*, Sociological Research Unit Monograph Series directed by Bernstein, B., London: Routledge & Kegan Paul, 1970).

6 Brandis, W. & Henderson, D., *Social Class, Language and Communication. (Primary Socialisation, Language and Education, Vol. I*, Sociological Research Unit Monograph Series directed by Bernstein, B., London: Routledge & Kegan Paul, 1970.)

7 Jesperson, O., *Mankind, Nation and Individual from a Linguistic Point of View* (Originally published 1946) Bloomington: Indiana University Press, 1964.

8 Whorf, B. L., *Language, Thought and Reality*, ed. Carroll, J. B. (Cambridge: M.I.T. Press, and New York: Wiley, 1956).

9 Murdock, G. P., *Social Structure* (New York: Macmillan, 1949).

10 Conklin, H. C., 'The relation of Hanunoo culture to the plant world'. Unpublished doctoral dissertation, Yale University, 1954.

11 Ravenette, A. T., 'Intelligence, personality and social class: an investigation into the patterns of intelligence and personality of working-class secondary school children'. Unpublished doctoral thesis, University of London, 1963.

12 Raven, J. C., *The Coloured Progressive Matrices* (London: Lewis, 1963).

13 Raven, J. C., *The Crichton Vocabulary Scale* (London: Lewis, 1951).

14 Brimer, M. A. & Dunn, L. M., *The English Picture Vocabulary Tests* (London: National Foundation for Educational Research, 1962).

15 Bereiter, C. & Engelmann, S., *Teaching Disadvantaged Children in the Preschool* (New Jersey: Prentice-Hall, 1966).

16 Neale, M. D. *Neale Analysis of Reading Ability* (London: Macmillan, 1958).

17 Douglas, op. cit. 2.

18 Barnard, B., *English Progress Test A2* (London: National Foundation for Educational Research, 1966).

19 Gahagan, G. A. & Gahagan, D. M., 'Paired-associate learning as partial validation of a language development program', *Child Developm.*, Vol. 39, No. 4, (1968), p. 1119.

20 Robinson, W. P. & Creed, C. D., 'Perceptual and verbal discriminations of "Elaborated" and "Restricted" code users', *Language & Speech*, Vol. 11, 3, (1968), p. 182-193.

21 Wallach, M. & Kogan, N., *Modes of Thinking in Young Children*, (New York: Holt Rinehart, 1965).

22 Barnard, op. cit. 18.

23 Douglas, op. cit. 2.

24 Bereiter, C. & Engelmann, S., op. cit. 15.

25 Jackson, B., 'The working class family', *The Sunday Times Magazine*, Nov. 10th, 1968.

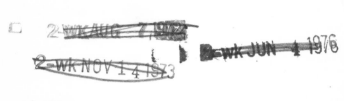